HOW TO PASS

HIGHER
ENGLISH

Ann Bridges

HODDER
GIBSON
PART OF HACHETTE UK

The Publishers would like to thank the following for permission to reproduce copyright material: 'Britain swings its hips to the salsa rhythm: From Latin to ballroom, a nation sheds its inhibitions, finds its feet and takes to the dancefloor' by Gerard Seenan, 20 March 2004, Copyright Guardian News & Media Ltd 2004; Extract from Big Bangs: Five Musical Revolutions by Howard Goodall, published by Chatto & Windus. Reprinted by permission of The Random House Group Ltd.

Questions from past exam papers are reproduced with kind permission of the Scottish Qualifications Authority.

Photo credits
p.5 © Randy M. Ury/Corbis; p.24 © Polak Matthew/Corbis Sygma; p.32 © Peter Johnson/Corbis; p.49 © BE&W agencja fotograficzna Sp. z o.o./Alamy; p.58 © Lester Lefkowitz/Corbis; p.92 © Lawrence Manning/Corbis; p.111 © Tom Grill/Corbis; p.121 © Colin Willoughby/Arena Images/Topfoto; p.123 © Mira/Alamy; p.127 © Owen Franken/Corbis.

Every effort has been made to trace all copyright holders, but if any have been inadvertently overlooked the Publishers will be pleased to make the necessary arrangements at the first opportunity.

Although every effort has been made to ensure that website addresses are correct at time of going to press, Hodder Gibson cannot be held responsible for the content of any website mentioned in this book. It is sometimes possible to find a relocated web page by typing in the address of the home page for a website in the URL window of your browser.

Hachette's policy is to use papers that are natural, renewable and recyclable products and made from wood grown in sustainable forests. The logging and manufacturing processes are expected to conform to the environmental regulations of the country of origin.

Orders: please contact Bookpoint Ltd, 130 Milton Park, Abingdon, Oxon OX14 4SB. Telephone: (44) 01235 827720. Fax: (44) 01235 400454. Lines are open 9.00–5.00, Monday to Saturday, with a 24-hour message answering service. Visit our website at www.hoddereducation.co.uk. Hodder Gibson can be contacted direct on: Tel: 0141 848 1609; Fax: 0141 889 6315; email: hoddergibson@hodder.co.uk

© Ann Bridges 2005, 2009
First published in 2005 by
Hodder Gibson, an imprint of Hodder Education,
Part of Hachette UK,
2a Christie Street
Paisley PA1 1NB

This colour edition first published 2009

Impression number 5 4 3
Year 2012 2011 2010

Cover photo © Photodisc
Cartoons © Moira Munro 2005, 2008
Typeset in 9.5pt Frutiger Light by Dorchester Typesetting Group Ltd
Printed in Italy

A catalogue record for this title is available from the British Library

ISBN-13: 978 0340 974 049

CONTENTS

An Introduction to Higher English v

PART 1   Paper 1: Close Reading

Chapter 1   Approach to Reading 3
       Overview 3
       Reading Paragraphs 11
       Reading Sentences 13

Chapter 2   Understanding 15
       Meaning 15
       Identifying Points 18
       Following Arguments and Tracing
          Developments 22
       Summarising a Number of Points 27
       Links 32

Chapter 3   Analysis 37
       Word Choice 40
       Imagery 45
       Structure 57
       Tone, Mood and Atmosphere 69
       Miscellaneous Techniques 78

Chapter 4   Evaluation 88
       Effectiveness of a Technique 88
       Effectiveness of an Example/Illustration/Anecdote... 90
       Effectiveness of a Conclusion 91
       Questions on Both Passages 93

Chapter 5   Timing – Close Reading 97
       Using Your Time Well in the Exam 97

PART 2   Paper 2: Critical Essay

Chapter 6   Critical Essay 101
       Welcome to the Critical Essay 101
       Becoming Familiar with the Exam Paper 103
       Becoming Familiar with the Questions 105

Chapter 7   Critical Essay Criteria 107
                    Essential Skills 107

Chapter 8   Mastering Your Text 110
                    Your Raw Materials 110
                    Organisation 111

Chapter 9   Selecting a Question 120
                    Drama 120
                    Poetry 122
                    Prose 124

Chapter 10 Understanding the Question and Selecting
                    Material 126
                    Drama Section 126
                    Prose Section – Fiction 130
                    Prose Section – Non-fiction 132
                    Poetry Section 134
                    Mass Media – Film and TV Drama Section 138
                    Language Section 142

Chapter 11 Writing Critical Essays 149
                    Planning Your Answer 149
                    Writing Your Essay 154

Chapter 12 How Many Texts? 160
                    Possible Options and their Effects 160

Chapter 13 How Many Quotations? 164
                    Choosing Quotations 164
                    Presenting Quotations 166

Chapter 14 Timing – Critical Essay 168
                    Using Your Time Well in the Exam 168

PART 3   Writing

Chapter 15 Writing – The Folio 172

AN INTRODUCTION TO HIGHER ENGLISH

Welcome to this Revision Book!

How to Pass Higher English. Does that mean how just to pass, to scrape through, Higher English? Or does it mean to pass as well as you can? This book will provide a few hints for the minimalists, but it should be much more useful to people who really want to give the exam their best shot.

It is not an idiot's guide to Higher English, because idiots are not the target audience. The targets are those of you who are prepared to do an honest job on their work in school or college, who are prepared to do (some) homework, and who want to do that little bit extra – or else you wouldn't even be thinking of buying this book. It will provide you with tips, but these are not short cuts so that you can avoid hard work.

Do you want to put the book back on the shelf right now? Or will you give it a go?

How to Use this Revision Book

We'll assume that you have decided to buy it. Start by looking at the Contents list. You will see that the book is organised into three sections: Close Reading, Critical Essay and Writing.

The book will not be concerned with the Units you do in your school or college. This book concentrates on the parts of the course which are externally assessed.

If you have bought this book near the beginning of your Higher year, you will find the examples in the Close Reading chapters hard. Don't worry about this. These are real Higher questions, and are meant to be dealt with when you are fighting fit, next May, not now when you are still getting to grips with the level of reading required. There is a training programme suggested for raising your reading fitness level to cope with Close Reading. There is a lot of detail, and some examples for you to try. Don't try to do them all at once. Grasp the principles behind each kind of question so that you can apply them to new, unseen questions on a new unseen topic.

The Critical Essay section does not provide a substitute for the teaching of texts. It tries to show you how you can use that teaching to the best advantage. Again, as in Close Reading, you may find that some of the material, especially in the spider diagrams and tables, is too complicated for you just now. Follow the advice about starting with the basics and moving on as you gain confidence.

Another thing to remember is that in English there is always a variety of acceptable answers to the questions. The answers in the book are good, but they are by no means the only possible ones.

PART 1

Paper 1: Close Reading

APPROACH TO READING

Not surprisingly the best preparation for a Close Reading paper is to read. But how much? How often? What is your reading history up to now? Which of the following words or phrases best describes your attitude to reading:

Voracious
Avid
Addicted
Mildly enthusiastic
Don't mind it
Will (if pushed)
Do I have to?
Cannae be bothered

If you come in any further down the scale than 'don't mind it' you have a problem. You can't make up for a misspent youth in three weeks. Your card playing skills may be great, but what about your reading skills?

You need a reading fitness programme – in fact almost everyone could benefit from this.

You do have to practise answering questions too, but you will not improve unless you can build your reading skills in general. Too often, when attempting practice papers you will do the same things well every time and make the same mistakes over and over again.

There are several forms of reading which you have to be skilful at, and which you must practise. We are going to look at:

◆ overview (reading the passage as a whole)

◆ reading paragraphs

◆ reading sentences.

Overview

The first skill you have to grasp is that of **overview**. You will make a more positive start on your first reading of a piece of prose if you know from the beginning what it is about. Newspapers use this technique when they put headlines and subheadings in an article. You will read on if the headline suggests that the subject might be of interest to you. It (and any subheadings or highlighted quotations from an article) will give you an idea of the kind of information which the article might contain.

Example 1

BRITAIN SWINGS ITS HIPS TO THE SALSA RHYTHM

From Latin to ballroom, a nation sheds its inhibitions, finds its feet and takes to the dance floor

> "You can stumble about without having to worry about looking cool"

> "It's blatant sexuality; it's what you need on a winter's night in Edinburgh"

These four items all stand out typographically in the article so that before you read it, you know that the subject will be a new fashion in dancing, that this dancing helps you lose your inhibitions and that it's friendly, social and has a sexy edge to it.

Hints and Tips

Your reading of the article will now be an *informed* reading because you know what to expect.

In the above paragraph the words 'inhibitions' and 'typographically' are words which you ought to recognise.

Example 2

FATHERS SPURN PLAN TO SAVE PARENTS FROM COURT BATTLES
Government unveils scheme to encourage mediation in contact rows

In this case you know to expect some explanation of an attempt to get (separated) parents to agree about contact times with children instead of going to court. You also know that some fathers don't think the plan will help them much. As a result you are on the lookout for what the plan is and the reasons why the fathers are against it. In other words you start your reading from a strong *informed* stance.

In the above paragraph you would be expected to know what 'spurn' and 'mediation' mean.

Fitness Training

You can train yourself to read an article effectively in order to obtain an overview of the information it contains. Like any other activity, if you want to succeed you have to go into training. Jogging and doing tummy curls are not seemingly all that relevant to getting your technique for a sprint start right, but you put up with it because you know that your general fitness and strength will improve. The same is true of reading: the detailed analysis techniques require different sets of skills to be exercised but your overall reading fitness has to come first.

Figure 1.1 Training is the key to success

If you already read most of a good daily paper or most of a heavy weekend paper, and read a couple of novels a month, with an occasional biography or historical/scientific text thrown in, then you don't need to read the next section. If, however, you do not fall into that category keep right on reading.

Daily Exercise

The most time-effective exercise – and time is probably short if you have just got round to reading this book – is to use *good quality journalism*. If you look back at past papers you will see the types of newspapers which provide sources for passages. There are extracts from books too, but the extracts tend to have the same kind of vocabulary level and the same kind of structures as good quality journalism.

1   Find an article which attracts you. (It might be because of the headline, the subject, or a photograph.)
2   Look at the headline, any subheadings and highlighted quotations, photo captions, etc.
3   Ask yourself 'What do I expect to find out by reading this?'
4   Read the article.
5   Ask 'What have I found out?'
6   Write down the main ideas, very briefly, in note form.

Now you have to be honest with yourself. (Nobody else is watching, after all.)

Ask 'How much did I understand at first reading? 100 per cent? 50 per cent? 25 per cent?'

If the answer is somewhere above 50 per cent give it another read and see if you gain any more information.

If the answer is less than 50 per cent is it because:

    a) You don't understand some of the words?
    b) You get lost in the line of thought?
    c) Both?

If a) is the problem, then get down to the article with a dictionary and look up the difficult words.

Now read the whole article again. Is the answer better than 50 per cent now? If it is, leave it there.

If b) is the problem, read each paragraph in turn and see how much you can get out of each paragraph.

Now read the whole article again. Is the answer better than 50 per cent now? If it is, leave it there.

If you are still not at the 50 per cent mark it might be helpful to give it another go, but you're probably heartily sick of it by now, so it's probably better just to leave it and try another one.

Repeat this exercise daily till the exam. Even though you don't feel that you are making progress, you will be. Like training for anything else, doing a little often is more effective than a big blitz just before the race.

Hints and Tips

If you want to make this exercise easier and less solitary, instead of writing down notes at the end of your reading, you could give the article to someone else after you have read it, and tell them what you think the main points are – long suffering parents, friendly adults, charitable elder brothers, even an intelligent dog will do. The important thing is that you are having to think and put your thoughts in words. If your 'sharer' comes up with other ideas and thoughts on your article, then so much the better (especially if it is the dog) but that is not really necessary.

Another word about training. If it doesn't hurt, it's not doing you any good. If you are sailing through the articles you choose, then you have to move on to articles with subject matter you know nothing about, or articles on subjects which you find boring. No pain, no gain.

Approach to Reading

Training Programme for Close Reading.

Preparation

Note down   Headline

```
┌─────────────────────────────────────────────────┐
│                                                 │
│                                                 │
│                                                 │
└─────────────────────────────────────────────────┘
```

Note down   Sub-headings

```
┌─────────────────────────────────────────────────┐
│                                                 │
│                                                 │
│                                                 │
│                                                 │
└─────────────────────────────────────────────────┘
```

What do I expect to find out from reading this article?

```
┌─────────────────────────────────────────────────┐
│                                                 │
│                                                 │
│                                                 │
└─────────────────────────────────────────────────┘
```

Action   Now, read the article.

Result   What have I found out? Write down the *main* ideas (in note form).

```
┌─────────────────────────────────────────────────┐
│                                                 │
│                                                 │
│                                                 │
│                                                 │
│                                                 │
│                                                 │
│                                                 │
└─────────────────────────────────────────────────┘
```

Evaluation   Did I find out what I expected?   Yes   No

How difficult was the reading?   Hard   OK   Easy

Fit for What?

Let's move on to find out how your practice can help you with the Higher Close Reading paper.

The passages are just like the articles you have been reading. They have the equivalents of headlines and subheadings, and your overview of them will be arrived at in the same way as you have in your practice.

Each passage in the Close Reading Paper has a short introduction before it starts. Each passage may also have a headline which will be highlighted by a typographic device (that is, they are in different print from the body of the article).

Here is an example from 2003.

Example 1

Passage 1

The first passage is an article in the Herald *newspaper in June 2002. In it, journalist and broadcaster Ruth Wishart offers some thoughts on attitudes to immigration to Scotland.*

CAN BRITAIN AFFORD TO KEEP TALENTED IMMIGRANTS OUT?

Passage 2

The second passage is adapted from an essay in the Guardian *newspaper, also in June 2002. In it, Anne Karpf explores past and present coverage of immigration issues and tells the story of one family from Kosovo who sought asylum in Britain.*

WE HAVE BEEN HERE BEFORE

The text in *italics* is an introduction, which gives you a clue as to what the article is going to be about.

In Passage 1, the important words are 'some thoughts on attitudes to immigration'. This is backed up by the headline in upper case (block capitals) which suggests that the writer will be on the side of more immigration.

In the second passage the important words are 'explores past and present coverage of immigration issues and tells the story of one family from Kosovo who…'

This is expanded by the headline which suggests that the past and present (press coverage) are not very different.

Hints and Tips

If you pay attention to these pieces of information before you start to read either of the articles, your first reading will be much more productive. You won't panic if some of the paragraphs or details appear to be too hard for you to understand, because you know roughly where you are going.

There is another aid to your general overview of the passages which is not present in newspapers, but which can help. After you have read the *two introductions* and the *two headlines* (if there are any) and, *before* you read the passages, look at the end of the paper at 'Questions on Both Passages'. This will often give you another clue about what you might find in the articles as a whole.

In this case the '**Question on Both Passages**' asks:

Which passage has given you a clearer understanding of key issues concerning immigration and asylum seeking?

This helps you to focus on what, overall, the passages will be about.

Noticing Tone

There is one more thing you can do at this stage which can help you onto the right track.

Try to **identify the tone** of each passage, in general terms, as you read. Is it serious, less than serious, funny, ironic, angry… ?

You can also use the introductions and the headlines to see if there are hints about the tone.

Example 2

Passage 1

In the first passage, Neil Ascherson, a distinguished journalist with the Observer *newspaper, considers society's attitude towards old age and old people.*

Passage 2

The second passage is taken from a collection of writing by mature women entitled New Ideas for Getting the Most Out of Life. *Here Mary Cooper explains how and why she intends to continue to grow old 'disgracefully'.*

Question on Both Passages

Identify the overall tone of each of the passages and say what effect the tone of each had on your appreciation of the passages.

On this occasion there are no headlines to help. From the introductions you know that both passages are concerned with old age: 'society's attitude to old age and old people' and an older woman's views on her own old age. You are also helped to see that there is a difference in tone between the two passages. Neil Ascherson is described as a 'distinguished' journalist, which suggests that his views will be given due weight by his readers. The use of the 'disgracefully' in inverted commas lets you know that Mary Cooper is not really intending to be disgraceful in the worst sense of the word. And the fact that you have been asked to talk about tone in the last question suggests that the tone of each passage is different. Probably the first passage will be serious and the second less so, perhaps even humorous.

Chapter 3 Analysis covers 'tone' much more closely (see pages 69–75) but it is useful to notice that even here, where you are reading for information – mainly concerned with Understanding – other aspects of the writing, in this case Tone, can help your overall reading of the passages, your overview.

Summary

Reading for overview of information.

1   Read the introduction to each passage. It's the part in italics.
2   Look at any headline given to each passage.
3   Read the Questions on Both Passages at the end of the paper.
4   Then ask 'What am I likely to find? What am I looking for in general terms?'
5   Then ask yourself 'Is there any hint as to the tone of the passage?'
6   Now, and only now, read the two passages.

This appears to take a long time and seems to prevent your getting started, but it only takes about two minutes. It's time well spent as it saves time by ensuring that your first reading is focused and productive.

Here are two examples for you to try. The first is from a newspaper; the second is from a past paper.

Example 1

Minimum wage comes of age

Now 16- and 17-year-olds qualify. But, as Philip Inman reports, unions fear a downside.

Driving down pay rates? Burger chains have reverted to age differentials between adult and younger workers.

? What do you expect to find out from reading this?

Answer on page 14 ➤

Example 2

Passage 1

Journalist Ian Wooldridge reflects on the life of Muhammed Ali in an article which appeared in the British Airways magazine High Life *in 2000.*

THE GREATEST VICTIM

Passage 2

The passage is adapted from the introduction to I'm a Little Special – a Muhammed Ali Reader. *Gerald Earley considers his feelings in the 1960s about his boyhood hero.*

THE GREAT ALI

Questions on Both Passages

From your reading of both passages, what do you think are the key reasons for Muhammed Ali's 'greatness'?

? **What do you expect to be important in each or both passages?**

Answer on page 14 ➤

Reading Paragraphs

Paragraphing is the writer's tool for giving you 'the story' in manageable chunks. It signals, for example, the introduction of a new idea, or a different way of expressing an idea which has previously been mentioned. It can be used to contain a conclusion, or the opening of another side to an argument, and for many other functions.

Topic Sentences

A paragraph usually has a **topic sentence**. It is often the first sentence, or at least near the beginning. This sentence tells you what the paragraph is going to be about, and it sometimes shows how this paragraph links with the one before.

Look at an example from the article about salsa dancing.

Example

The 7.15 Latin dance class is full, as was the six o'clock, as is the 8.30. In the reception area of Edinburgh Dancebase, learners, ranging from the middle aged, fresh from work, to students, mill around waiting to dance.

The topic of this paragraph is that dance classes in Edinburgh are full.

Unlikely as it may at first seem, this is occurring across the country. Against similar winter backdrops people are queuing up to learn to dance. National inhibition is being shed as

Example continued ➤

Example *continued*

salsa, merengue and cumbia beats force hips to sway rhythmically and partners to twist complicatedly. French ceroc classes are filling up, street dancing to hip hop is being used as an exercise class. Even ballroom dancing is enjoying something of a renaissance.

The topic of this paragraph is full dance classes are occurring all across the country. What follows is simply a list of the kinds of dance classes which are popular.

Because of the popularity of partner dancing – as opposed to the lone experience of shuffling one's feet and randomly jerking your arms at a club/family wedding – the BBC has decided to make a celebrity version of *Come Dancing* the centrepiece of its new Saturday night schedule. Fronted by Bruce Forsyth, the show will feature celebrities testing their salsa skills under the guidance of world champion ballroom dancer Donnie Burns.

The important idea in this paragraph is 'The BBC has decided to make a celebrity version of Come Dancing…' *What follows simply describes what the programme will contain.*

Now you have three paragraphs which have informed you of the three steps in an **argument** about dancing.

1   Dance classes in Edinburgh are full.
2   This is happening all over the country.
3   (It is so popular) the BBC is going to showcase this kind of dancing.

Key Words *and* Definitions

Argument is used here in its academic or literary sense – it does not mean an argument as in a fight or disagreement. It means the structure or framework of a discussion on a topic.

Hints *and* Tips

The beauty of being able to perform this paragraph exercise quickly is that it allows you to see what is important in the discussion without having to become bogged down in the details. However, in order to be able to do this, you have to practise. It's obviously something that you could take in as an extension to your daily training exercise. Choose two or three paragraphs in a row and try to identify the topic of each and see how they link together in the argument.

Summary

1   Identify the topic sentence or main idea in each paragraph.
2   Look at a sequence of these paragraphs and see how the argument of the article is developing.

Reading Sentences

Sometimes you have to deal with a sentence – particularly a long and complex one – in the same way as a paragraph. You have to find out what the important or main idea of the sentence is. What is it supposed to be telling you about? You should be able to identify the 'subject' of the sentence. The **subject** is the thing or person the sentence is going to tell you about.

Here is a typical long sentence:

Example

Because of the popularity of partner dancing – as opposed to the lone experience of shuffling one's feet and randomly jerking your arms at a club/family wedding – the BBC has decided to make a celebrity version of *Come Dancing* the centrepiece of its new Saturday night schedule.

? What is the subject here, and what are we being told about it?

The first thing you can do to simplify the sentence for yourself is to ignore the part between the two dashes for the moment – the part 'in parenthesis'.

So the sentence becomes: 'Because of the popularity of partner dancing the BBC has decided to make a celebrity version of *Come Dancing* the centrepiece of its new Saturday night schedule.'

'The BBC' is the subject and what you are told about it is that it has decided to do a show on dancing. The rest of the sentence gives you more information about this fact. It tells us why they are going to do it (partner dancing is popular) and it also tells us a bit about why partner dancing is popular (because it's better than shuffling on your own) but the important idea is that 'the BBC has decided to put on a dancing programme'.

Summary

1 Try to identify the main 'subject' of the sentence.

2 Note what are you being told about the main subject.

3 To simplify the sentence you can (temporarily) ignore parts in parenthesis, or long lists of similar items.

Answers

Example 1 (page 10)

16- and 17-year-olds now will get a minimum wage guaranteed. This seems to be good news but unions don't like it because it might upset the pay rates that some people have already been getting.

Example 2 (page 11)

Passage 1 is going to give a biography of Ali, probably showing difficulties he was up against.

Passage 2 is going to be about the things Ali did which created hero worship in the boy.

Both are going to be concerned with the things he did which made him seem 'great', despite the difficulties.

The tone of the second piece might be personal, affectionate, admiring.

Chapter 2

UNDERSTANDING

In the Close Reading Paper **Codes** are used to identify the kinds of questions you are being asked to tackle. Three letters are used **U**, **A** and **E**. In this first section we are going to look at Understanding questions – the ones coded **U**. These questions fall into five recognisable types, each of which asks for a slightly different approach.

1 Meaning

2 Identifying points

3 Following arguments and tracing developments

4 Summarising a number of points

5 Links

What You Should Know

The Understanding questions in the paper are designed to be helpful. (Honestly!) They make sure that you look closely at words or phrases, sentences and paragraphs. Even if your answer is not wholly accurate, you will have been forced to pay attention to the parts of the passages which are most important for your overall grasp of the ideas.

1 Meaning

This is the simplest type of Understanding question **if** you recognise the words or phrases that are being asked about. How many words you will recognise depends on your past reading history.

This kind of question usually starts with one of the following:

Hints and Tips

There is no magic wand to substitute for a sustained reading habit – the only way now is to read, read, and read some more. (See training programme pages 4–7.)

◆ Explain what the writer means by…

◆ Explain the significance of the word…

◆ Show how you are helped towards the meaning of…

◆ How does the context help you to understand the meaning of…

◆ Explain this expression in your own words…

2 Identifying Points

This type of Understanding question is one where you want to make the most of your chances, because it is usually quite straightforward.

It is the kind of question which starts with something like:

◆ What are the three reasons for...

◆ What four things, in their view, do they expect...

◆ What three main reasons does the writer give for...

◆ What other ways of looking at education are laid out...

Look at these examples to see what is involved.

Example 1

The BBC is a massive patron, uniquely independent through its licence fee – and the guardian of public service broadcasting. But, as the fight for the control of communications hots up, friends of the BBC – both inside and out – are alarmed that all this is in jeopardy: the BBC has become too much of a self-seeking institution, too preoccupied with its ratings at the expense of good broadcasting, and unwisely over-extended financially.

What are the three reasons for causing alarm to the friends of the BBC? Use your own words as far as possible. 3U

This is quite an easy example. You can see where the idea 'are alarmed' is in the paragraph. Then there is a colon, which tells you that there is going to be an explanation following, and there are two commas dividing the explanation into three parts. These three parts are going to give you your answer.

1 The BBC has become too much of a self-seeking institution

2 ... too preoccupied with its ratings at the expense of good broadcasting

3 ... unwisely over-extended financially.

Common Mistakes

However, if you simply write these three things down as your answer you will score very few (if any) marks. Why?

Well, this is an Understanding question: it has 3U at the side. So you have to show that you understand what these three reasons are. That means putting these reasons into *your own words* as far as possible.

Take reason number **1**. Obviously there is no simpler way of saying 'The BBC has become too much of a' so you can leave this if you want to. What you must 'translate' or paraphrase is the phrase 'self-seeking institution'. So your answer will be something like: 'The BBC is an *organisation* which had become too concerned with *looking after its own interests*. (Or, '... its own importance/advantage/ aggrandisement.')

You have shown by this answer that you understand the two 'difficult' ideas:

institution = organisation

self-seeking = looking after its own interests

Let us now follow the same process with reason number **2**. Here we probably want to put in our own words 'preoccupied', 'ratings', 'expense' and 'broadcasting'.

'The BBC was too *concerned* with its *viewing figures* at the **cost** of good *programming*.'

This 'translates' correctly, and would gain full marks, but so would the answer 'The BBC was too concerned about viewing figures *to care much* about good programming.' This answer shows full understanding without having mechanically translated 'expense'.

Reason number **3** involves the same process.

The BBC had *foolishly* (unwisely) *spent too much* (over-extended) *money* (financially).

It has probably taken you a lot longer to read this section than you would actually spend writing your answer. But how should you write down your answer so that it is quick for you and clear to the marker?

Here is one common way:

'The BBC was an organisation which had become too concerned with looking after its own interests, it was too concerned about viewing figures to care much about good programming and it had foolishly borrowed too much money.'

Another way would be to put each reason in a different line, just to make it perfectly clear where one reason ends and another starts.

The BBC was an organisation which had become too concerned with looking after its own interests.

It was too concerned about viewing figures to care much about good programming.

It had foolishly borrowed too much money.

You might even number these points (or bullet point them). There is absolutely no need to do this unless it helps you to be clear in your own mind that you have found and dealt with three separate reasons.

Example 2

In my experience, most people in the Arctic who direct the activities of employees, who seek to streamline the process of resource extraction without regard to what harm might be done to the land, do so with the idea that their goals are desirable and admirable, and that they are shared by everyone. They believe they are working in this way 'for the common good'. In their view the working man must provide cheerful labour, be punctual, and demonstrate allegiance to the concept of a greater good orchestrated from above. The Inuit, for his part, must conduct himself either as a sober and aspiring middle-class wage earner or, alternatively, as an 'authentic', traditional 'Eskimo', that is, according to an idealised and unrealistic caricature, created by the outsider. The land, the very ground itself, the plants and the animals, must also produce something – petroleum, medicines, food, the setting for a movie – if is it is to achieve any measure of worth. If it does not, it is waste. Tundra wasteland. A waste of time. (lines 1–12)

? The employers in the Arctic believe that they are working for 'the common good'.

What four things, in their view, do they expect to support them in their goals?

4U

The phrase 'in their view' alerts you to the fact that the answers will probably lie after that phrase in the paragraph – from line 5 to the end.

Again, as in the previous example, the sentence structure will help you to pick out these things.

Logically, our thinking should follow this train of thought:

◆ We might reasonably expect there to be one sentence for each reason.

◆ But here we have only three sentences: one about the 'working man'; one about the 'Inuit'; and one about 'the land'.

◆ So one of the sentences must contain two separate ideas.

◆ The phrase 'or, alternatively' is one of those phrases which alerts you to links and changes in the course of an argument.

◆ Therefore there are probably two ideas in the middle sentence about the Inuit.

The answer will have to take each of these four sections and state in your own words what the employers expect. However, in this case, you are dealing with whole sentences, each with quite a number of words, and you are only being offered 4 marks so you don't have to 'translate' every hard word (although you may do that if you like). It is more likely that you are being required to give the gist or overall impression of each of the sections you have identified.

The employers expect that:

◆ The working man should do his job efficiently and without question.

◆ The Inuit should behave like obedient workers anxious to please.

◆ They could provide 'local colour' by portraying the expected stereotype.

◆ The land is there to be exploited for all its products.

As you can see, in this kind of question you have to do two things.

1 Identify the part of the paragraph/sentence/phrase which contains each of the reasons/attitudes/changes/factors.

2 Show that you know what each means by using your own words (translating/paraphrasing/recasting) in your answer.

Example 3

The urge to write may also be the fear of death – particularly with autobiography – the need to leave messages for those who come after, saying, 'I was here; I saw it too'. Then there are the other uses of autobiography, some more utilitarian than others – exposure, confession, revenge. In writing my first volume of autobiography 'Cider with Rosie', I was moved by several of these needs, but the chief one was celebration: to praise the life I'd had and so preserve it.

? **What three main reasons does Laurie Lee give for writing autobiography in lines 1–6?**   3U

The three reasons are wanting to:

◆ record history or personal experience in some way

◆ use the autobiography to settle old scores or to justify oneself

◆ tell everyone about the joyfulness of his life, and/or to remind himself about it.

If you chose to translate 'exposure', 'confession' and 'revenge' you would only get 1 mark. Technically you are right – these *are* three reasons for writing autobiography; but there are two clues in the question which should show you that this is not the *whole* answer.

The first clue is 'three **main** reasons' and the second is 'does Laurie Lee give ... **in lines 1–6**?'

> You should not be satisfied with an answer which deals with such a small part of the paragraph. Look *throughout* the line references you have been given.

What You Should Know

1 Make sure you are looking at the correct section of the passage. You will always be given a line reference (for example, lines 23–31). There is nothing worse than writing a brilliant answer only to find later that you have gone too far in the passage so that only half of it is relevant.

2 Use your 'own words'. There will often be an instruction to 'Use your own words as far as possible' in the question itself, but even if there isn't, you are expected to do it anyway. An important instruction is quite clearly stated on the very first page of your exam paper – the page you *must* read even though you are in such a hurry to get started.

Use your own words whenever possible and particularly when you are instructed to do so.

If you don't use your own words, if you simply 'lift' or quote straight from the passage, the marker of your paper is told to give you **0 marks**.

3 Following Arguments and Tracing Developments

Following Arguments

In this kind of question you could be asked to look at a sentence (probably a long, complex one), or a paragraph, or a section of the passage involving two or three paragraphs, or even the whole of one of the passages. The purpose of this kind of question is to see if you can understand and recognise the line of thought through a section of the passage. The good news is that you can do this without understanding every word in the section; the bad news is that you have to be able to follow complex sentences and paragraphs.

Questions of this kind usually have the word 'explain' or 'explanation' somewhere in them, or sometimes even just 'Why?'

Here is quite an easy example:

Example 1

Scots nationalism has always been on the defensive. It emerged, the first nationalism in Christian Europe to be fully conscious of itself, when Scotland was in desperate danger of total conquest and political obliteration by a stronger neighbour. For centuries Scots had to fight bitterly and almost continuously for the mere chance to remain Scottish. They were poor, few, and remote from the great centres of European life. The source of the pride was simply this, that, in spite of everything, they had contrived to remain themselves.

Read this paragraph carefully (lines 1–6).

Explain in your own words what was the origin of Scottish national pride. 2U

You might be tempted to read this question as a 'translation' question and deal with the last sentence. The 'source' is after all the 'origin'. So you might say 'in spite of the difficulties they had managed to maintain their identity'. In some ways this is a good enough answer, and certainly worth half marks. But you were asked to read the **whole** paragraph, so you are expected to use some of the material from that paragraph in your answer. In this case, it would probably be a good idea to mention some of the difficulties, such as the possibility of being taken over by England, the fact that they were a country with few resources, and they only just managed to survive as a nation. This answer would gain full marks, and there is the added bonus that you do not have to know what 'contrived' means.

Example 2

In a generation, living to 100 will be common. Society is still utterly unprepared for this change. Chatter about 'grey power', or even the growing and admirable concern for the old and helpless who are not cared for by families, have scarcely touched the problem. The old, still veiled in outworn stereotypes and new-fangled prejudice, are the Great Excluded.

? **By referring to lines 1–4, explain fully the difficulties that such longevity causes.**

2U

Your first difficulty here is with the question itself. Do you know the meaning of the word 'longevity'? If you don't, or can't guess it from its context, then you are not going to be able to answer this question. This goes back to the statement in the Introduction about your general vocabulary level and fitness to sit Higher English. The examiner obviously thinks that you should know (or be able to guess from the context) what 'longevity' means.

As the paragraph is about old people ('living to 100 will be common') the word presumably means a long life span, living until one is very old. Having solved that problem, you can now get down to the answer.

'We as a society are not ready to deal with all the old people who will be alive in the twenty-first century and although there is a vague understanding of the potential difficulties, the old are not catered for yet in the thinking of planners of our social system.'

Here, you have 'explained fully' because you have covered all of the lines in the question (see page 22). You have also avoided having to translate 'veiled in outworn stereotypes' which would be quite hard, but you have shown understanding of the main ideas of the paragraph.

Here is another example for you to try.

Example 3

(This is from a passage about the Scots sense of identity: it follows on from Example 1 (see page 22)).

. . . the source of the pride was simply this, that, in spite of everything, they had contrived to remain themselves.

In later centuries, when the political rights of nationality had been sacrificed, first in part, then almost completely, the Scotsman's most obvious means of asserting his country's continued existence was to insist on its separateness, the uniqueness of Scottish scenes and Scottish customs. Human nature being what it is, this meant that, almost inevitably, he would also be found insisting that those things in Scotland in which he took particular pride were the best of their kind in the world.

Read lines 3–8.

Using your own words, explain why and in what ways this pride changed in later centuries.

3U

Answer on page 36 ➤

Tracing Developments

Another way of asking this kind of question is to ask you to show the development of a word or idea.

Often the idea in question will be from the topic sentence of a paragraph, so you would expect the paragraph to go on to give you a more detailed or expanded version of the topic.

Hints and Tips

It is important to look at the line references you are given in this kind of question.

There will be a limit given as to how far you have to trace the development. This is necessary because any idea from the beginning of a passage is probably going to be developed right through to the end, so you need to know where to stop your answer.

Figure 2.1 Scottish national pride

In the first example you should notice that the section you are asked to deal with is very small.

Example 1

(This passage deals with an atomic waste disposal site.)

As a condition for permitting the site to go ahead, the U.S. Congress has insisted that a warning sign should be erected when it closes down. This would have to be capable of alerting future generations to the risk of opening up this unwanted tomb. It would be the most momentous 'Keep Out' sign in history, a statement so forceful that it would drive people – or any other form of intelligent life – away from the area until AD 12,000.

How is the idea contained in the word 'momentous' developed in the rest of that sentence? (lines 3–5)   2U

In order to answer this question you obviously have to have some idea of what 'momentous' means. If you don't know you have to do some quick thinking.

1   It should have something to do with 'moment'.

2   'Moment' means a very short space of time, a second. This would give a meaning to most momentous as something like the shortest. In the context this doesn't make sense – if anything it should be the longest.

3   So what does the context suggest? 'so forceful it would drive away' – something to do with strength, then?

4   Is there another meaning of moment? In the phrase 'It is a matter of great moment that…' the word means 'importance'. This fits much better.

If you have done all that work, you are now in a position to answer the question.

The idea of 'momentous' is developed by saying that the sign has to do something really important – keeping everyone away from the place for thousands of years. And not just human beings, but any other form of life.

Even if you had only got as far as Stage 3 in your understanding of the meaning of 'momentous' you could still have written some kind of reasonable answer.

Example 2

(The previous paragraph has given statistics about the large increase in the life expectancy figures.)

The figures don't add up to an unmixed disaster scenario. Unless the economy collapses, British governments during the next generation can perfectly well afford to go on paying the present levels of state old-age pension, and could almost certainly afford to raise it in terms of real income. The problem here is political will rather than financial capacity. The pinch will come in other resource areas, such as health spending. People over 65 consume three times as many prescription items as other age groups. Nearly half of those with some measure of disability are over 70.

(?) 'The figures don't add up to an unmixed disaster scenario.'

Explain the meaning of this sentence. Go on to explain how the ideas of the sentence are developed in the rest of the paragraph. **4U**

The first part of this question is done as set out on page 16.

You have to translate 'unmixed disaster scenario'. A disaster scenario is a set of circumstances in which you expect only dramatically unfortunate events to happen. Unmixed suggests that there will be no mixing of good with this bad. But the sentence says that this is not so 'It does not add up to'. So the first part of your answer might be:

The bad consequences of these statistics will not be completely overwhelming. There are better aspects also. (**2 marks**)

(!) **Danger!**

Because you have just spent some time and thought on writing your answer to the first part of the question, you might forget that there is another sentence.

Always make sure how many parts there are to a question, and do all that you are asked to do.

The second part of the question is to do with the **development** of this idea.

Part of the paragraph suggests that things are not going to be as bad as thought:

In economic terms the government can afford to cope with all these old people. The paragraph then goes on to say that despite that there are still some negative aspects like the burden on the health service. (**2 marks**)

Here you have shown the 'not unmixed' (that is, the 'mixed') nature showing both positive and negative aspects.

(⇨) **Here is an example for you to try.**

Example 3

(*This is from a passage about the influence of screen violence.*)

The question of media influence is properly understood as an environmental issue. At a time when we are demanding that industry takes more responsibility for its pollution of our air and our water, it's entirely appropriate to insist that Hollywood and its like demonstrate greater accountability for their pollution of the cultural atmosphere we breathe.

? By referring to lines 1–4 show how the writer develops his statement that media influence is 'an environmental issue'.   2U

Answer on page 36 ➤

Summary

1   Take account of all the material within the line references.
2   'Explain fully' suggests that you don't just stop at the first idea – follow through to the end of the section you have been given.

4 Summarising a Number of Points

This kind of question is one where you can pile up marks quickly if you think a little before dashing into your answer. Often these questions come quite near the end so you may feel pushed for time.

Another identifying feature of these questions is that they usually ask you to look at quite a long section of the passage (often two or three paragraphs) and usually there are at least 3, sometimes as many as 5, marks available for the answer.

There are several ways of asking this kind of question and they can demand slightly different approaches.

1   Identify five benefits…
2   Outline briefly the main effects…
3   Briefly summarise the main points…
4   Summarise the main reasons…
5   What do you think are the key reasons…

And there are other possibilities.

Hints and Tips

A good practice with this kind of question is to see what you are looking for before you embark on the reading of what could be a quite lengthy extract. This leads to a more informed and purposeful reading (see page 4).

Here is an example covering the types of question (1–3) in the list above. They are quite straightforward.

Example 1

Our gaze now shifts much nearer in the time corridor – to the invention of recorded sound. Though the early gramophone came into being in the 1870s as a result of the desire to record and reproduce speech, very soon its principal, almost monogamous marriage was with music./ **1** Thomas Alva Edison's invention of recorded sound unleashed on the twentieth century a massive amount of music in a multitude of forms; / **2** it gave music wings to cross the planet. / **3** Before the gramophone age, people heard a particular piece of orchestral music maybe once or twice a decade. Now anything can be listened to, instantly, at the flick of a switch, the drop of a needle or the aiming of a laser. / **4** 150 years ago the very slowness of making a notated score of a piece of music meant that the creator had to live with it and think about it for a period of time before it was released to the world. Now a recording can be made instantaneously, even at the point of creation. / **5** Where once a catchy, impulsive melody made up on the spot and enjoyed for the evening would die the next morning never to be heard again, now everything can be captured for posterity. / **6** And in addition, where once musicians lived and died on their live performance, now editing allows them to relive and redo their mistakes and wobbles as many times as they like.

? Consider lines 1–16.

Using your own words as far as possible, identify five benefits the gramophone has brought to the world of music.   5U

This is really quite an easy question, but in your rush to get down the details you might miss something or confuse two ideas into one, or some other error. One way of approaching this question is to section off each benefit as you see it happen in the list.

This has been done for you in the example above.

Now you simply have to choose five of these and put each of them in your own words.

Answer

[1]Own words – The gramophone allowed lots of music to be transmitted to the people of the twentieth century.

[2]Own words – It allowed music to move all across the world.

[3]Own words – Any piece of music can be listened to exactly where and when you want to hear it.

[4]Own words – A composer can record his compositions immediately instead of writing them down first.

[5]Own words – Spontaneous music can be preserved for later listening.

[6]Own words – Musicians can have their best performances recorded with no mistakes thanks to editing.

This gives you a very quick five marks. All you have to do is:

1 Write your sentences so that they flow on from one another and form a paragraph.

Or

2 List your sentences as bullet points.

Or

3 Number your sentences and list them.

In the above answer we have six benefits, but it is probable that at least one of the original sentences might have presented you with difficulties. For example, if you didn't feel sure about what 'gave music wings to cross the planet' meant you might not have felt sure about number [2], but you know you have five others. Or perhaps you didn't know what 'posterity' meant in sentence [5], so you might have missed that one out and still had five others.

Hints and Tips

The advantage of starting by marking the sentences in the passage is that you can see clearly where the possible answers are, and you won't fall into the trap of repeating yourself or confusing two ideas. It stops you, for example, from taking sentence [3] and making that three separate benefits, flicking a switch, dropping a needle, aiming a laser.

Here is an example of the last two types of question (4 and 5) on the list on page 27. They are more difficult because you are asked about reasons rather than just points or facts. This kind of question is more difficult to answer with a simple list of bullet points. Because you are being asked about 'reasons' there will probably have to be some linking in your answer to create an explanation rather than just a series of facts.

Example 2

And mainstream America's rejection? / [1] He was a national hero on return to Louisville from his Olympic triumph, but there were still those who called him 'boy' and restaurants which didn't admit blacks. / [2] Disillusioned, his riposte was to jettison the name Cassius Clay, handed down from the slave owners of his African forebears, and become Muhammed Ali, pilgrim of Mecca, convert to the Muslim faith. It was a predictable decision but one which was to bring opprobrium upon him nationwide. / [3] To much of middle-class America he was now a renegade and soon became a pariah when he refused the draft to fight for his country in Vietnam. /'I ain't got no quarrel with them Vietcong,' he said. And was subsequently, at the peak of his career, banned from boxing for four years.

I am not a boxing expert. Those who are, mostly endorse Muhammed Ali's opinion of himself at his peak: 'The Greatest.' But it took a long time for mainstream America to become reconciled to that judgement. / [4] For many he was a turbulent, disturbing figure who challenged homespun values.

(?) Summarise the main reasons for 'mainstream America's rejection' of Muhammed Ali. You should use your own words as far as possible.　　　　5U

(!) **Before starting this question, do you know, or can you guess, the meanings of disillusioned, riposte, jettison, predictable, opprobrium, renegade, pariah, turbulent, homespun? You should know at least half of them if you are to have any chance of success in this question. (More training required?)**

If we try to section off reasons why Ali was rejected, we get something like the four sections marked in the passage above. It is not quite so neat as the 'list' we had for the previous question, and each item is not at all straightforward. We are being asked for reasons, not facts, so let's take each bit section by section.

Answer

[1]We can deduce from this sentence that: Ali was rejected **because** racial prejudice was common at the time.

[2]There is more deduction to be done here: Ali was rejected **because** he changed his name from an 'American' one to a Muslim one and this was seen as a betrayal of America and its values.

[3]Another main reason for his rejection was **because** he refused to fight for America in the Vietnam War and people considered his refusal made him a traitor.

[4]He didn't fit in with the nice cosy set of family values so much accepted by most Americans, **so** they felt uncomfortable about him.

There is the material we need for the answer. It would be a good answer, which would probably get 5 marks, but it could be made more convincing by linking the ideas together.

Answer

Ali was rejected because racial prejudice was common at the time. Ali was **further** rejected because he changed his name from an 'American' one to a Muslim one and this was seen as a betrayal of America and its values. **An even more powerful reason** for his rejection was when he refused to fight for America in the Vietnam War. People considered his refusal made him a traitor. **Overall** he didn't fit in with the nice cosy set of family values accepted by most Americans so they felt uncomfortable about him.

You can't get 6 marks for this because it is only a 5 mark question, but you are convincing the marker that you know what you are doing. And that is not a bad idea.

Here is an example for you to try.

Example 3

All this because, says the Intergovernmental Panel on Climate Change, temperatures could rise by as much as 6 degrees Centigrade in the 21st century, ten times as fast as temperatures have risen in the last 100 years. Who will want to live in such a world – especially in some of the regions likely to be hardest hit, which happens to include those already the poorest on the planet? Dry areas will get drier, wet areas will get wetter. Africa will suffer in ways that scientists cannot fully predict, but the Sahel will probably become drier and more prone to drought and famine than it already is. For Europe, it will mean the influx of such pathogens as malaria, dengue fever and encephalitis as warmer weather encourages the northern movement of disease-carrying mosquitoes. Generally warmer weather can more easily harbour cholera and other waterborne diseases which will be more easily spread during frequent floods.

Some argue that the ultimate result of global warming will be a paradoxical but even more catastrophic global cooling. As the Arctic ice cap melts, a flow of fresh water into the North Atlantic could disrupt conveyer currents including the Gulf Stream, which is what keeps northern Europe warm. According to Steve Hall, oceanographer at Southampton Oceanography centre, 'One moment we could be basking in a Mediterranean climate and the next icebergs could be floating down the English Channel.' It would take just one quarter of 1% more fresh water flowing into the North Atlantic from melting Arctic glaciers to bring the northwards flow of the Gulf Stream to a halt.

? In these lines the writer describes the possible effects of global warming. Using your own words as far as possible, outline briefly the main effects on Africa, on Europe and on the North Atlantic. 5U

Answer on page 36 ➤

Hints and Tips

The formula for answering this kind of question is to identify in the linking sentence *two* words or phrases, one pointing *back* and one pointing *forward*. You then have to link the *backward* pointing one with the relevant part of *the previous paragraph*, and the *forward* pointing one you have to link with the relevant parts of *the following paragraph*.

This really is a formula which you can apply almost as if it were a mathematical formula. If it helps to think in terms of *x* and *y*, or to colour code, then why not?

Example 2

This week the Home Secretary was assuring his French counterpart that Britain would clamp down even more severely on those working here illegally. At the same time plans are advanced for 'accommodation centres', which will have the immediate effect of preventing natural integration. Meanwhile, ever more sophisticated technology is to be employed to stem the numbers of young men who risk their lives clinging to the underside of trains.

Yet at the heart of **this ever more draconian approach** to immigration policy lie a **number of misconceptions**. The UK is not a group of countries swamped by a tidal wave of immigrants. Relatively speaking Europe contends with a trickle of refugees compared with countries who border areas of famine, desperate poverty or violent political upheaval.

? Referring to specific words or phrases, show how the sentence 'Yet...misconceptions' performs a linking function in the writer's line of thought.

2U

Answer

'**this ever more draconian approach**' refers back to **the harsh measures** which are to be taken against immigrants mentioned in the first paragraph. The '**number of misconceptions**' is illustrated in the rest of the paragraph where it talks about the **mistakes that people make** in their assumptions about immigrants.

This answer has covered all four parts necessary to get full marks.

Here is an example for you to try.

This passage is about the problems of old age.

Example 3

The problem here is political will rather than financial capacity. The pinch will come in other resource areas, such as health spending. People over 65 consume three times as many prescription items as other age groups. Nearly half of those with some measure of disability are over 70.

But the resource question, meeting the material needs of the old and elderly, is only half the story. The real problem lies elsewhere – in the imagination. What are the old for? Who are they, and do traditional divisions of human life into childhood, youth, middle-age and old-age still fit our experience?

(?) Referring to specific words or phrases, explain how the sentence 'But...story' acts as a link in the writer's line of thought. 2U

Answer on page 36 ➤

In all of these examples you have been told that the sentence acts as a link. The question could be rephrased in such a way that you had to recognise that what you were being asked about is the link question.

Example 4

(?) 'What is the function of the sentence in the argument of this passage. By referring closely to specific words and phrases show how it fulfils this function. 3U

This probably is a link question, and your first mark out of the three would be for identifying the function as a linking one, and the other two would be earned in the same way as the examples you have looked at.

(!) But beware, the sentence might have some other function – so look carefully to see if it is a link.

Summary

1   Remember that link answers usually should have **four** specific parts.

Answers

Example 3 (page 17)

The Inuit feel afraid about it and they find it unbelievable that we should want to do it.

'**Apprehension**' and '**incredulity**' have been translated and related to the feelings of the Inuit.

An answer which merely put down: 'Fear and disbelief' would gain very little credit because although the translation is correct the question hasn't been answered.

Example 4 (page 17)

'Monstrous verbosity' means an appalling number of worthless words. 'Five words where one would do' shows that there were too many words (and the phrases quoted such as 'in-plant feeding station' show how pointless the words are).

A correct meaning is given in the first sentence so 1 mark is secure. The second mark is given for a correct use of context. The answer would probably have been sufficient even if it had stopped at 'too many words'.

Example 3 (page 24)

Scottish political rights and independence disappeared over the centuries, and as a result of this the Scots had to fall back on boasting about the things they still had which were purely Scottish – the scenery and cultural habits – to give them a sense of their own nationality.

Example 3 (page 27)

He develops the idea by showing that we demand that the pollution caused by industry should be controlled because it damages the environment, so we should also demand that pollution in films (scenes of violence) should be controlled because it damages our society's ideas and attitudes.

Example 3 (page 31)

Parts of Africa will become drier.

Europe will suffer from mosquito-borne diseases and waterborne diseases because of the floods.

The north Atlantic will become colder and will divert the course of the Gulf stream southwards.

Example 3 (page 35)

The 'resource question' refers back to the problems of funding health care for the elderly, 'is only half the story' points forward to the rest of the paragraph which is going to look at the other half of the story – the real problems of identity in old age.

ANALYSIS

All the work we have done so far has been concerned with Understanding. If you have a reasonable vocabulary, and if you have been practising reading for information and understanding, experience says that you will do reasonably well in the Understanding questions. Most people make proportionally more marks in these questions than in the Analysis ones.

However, you can learn how to do Analysis questions as well. Make sure you are absolutely clear on what you are being asked to do. Remember that in an Analysis question it is *unlikely* that you will be being asked merely to explain *meaning*. If that were the case, the question would be marked U.

Key Points

There are four pointers to what kind of question you are being asked:

1   The use of the letter **A** to remind you that analysis is required.

2   The naming of a particular **feature or technique** in the question, for example:

Show how the writer uses **imagery** in lines x–y to emphasise the impact of…

3   The instruction to look at a section and then 'Show how…' with a **list of possible features** which you might try, for example:

Show how the writer conveys his feelings in lines x–y. In your answer you may refer to **tone, point of view, onomatopoeia, imagery, or any other appropriate language feature**.

4   The instruction to look at the writer's **use of language** and 'Show how…', for example:

Show how the writer's **use of language** in lines x–y highlights the importance of…

In this last case there is no named technique or feature to guide you. You must go through your own mental list of techniques and see which you can identify as being important, before you can start your answer. You would probably consider more than one feature.

Common Mistakes

In the fourth type of question, people sometimes make the mistake of assuming that **language** simply equals *meaning* and paraphrase the lines to show that they have understood them. This will get **0 marks** because it ignores two important instructions:

◆   The **A** at the end of the question

◆   '**Show how**…' something works.

Reading Questions Carefully

Once you have identified the question as one of the above types you then have to look carefully at the question to decide how many techniques or features you have to deal with.

1 Sometimes a question will say 'Show how the writer uses **word choice** in…'

This is a simple instruction which you are unlikely to get wrong.

2 Another question might say 'Show how the writer uses word choice **and** sentence structure in…'

Again, this is relatively simple: You have to find examples of both techniques.

3 Yet another question might say 'Show how the writer uses imagery **or** tone to…'

Here you have a choice to make but you will only do one.

4 Or, the question might say 'Show how the writer uses imagery **and/or** tone to…'

Here you can do either one technique or both.

5 Or, finally, the question might say 'Show how features of the writer's language…' (Watch for the use of the **plural** here in '**features**'; you would have to tackle more than one feature.)

In the examination paper these key words are normally not put in bold lettering, you are supposed to be able to read carefully to find out what it is you have to do.

Why don't all analysis questions say either, 'Do word choice' or 'Do tone', without having all these alternatives?

◆ In the simple cases, the lines you are being asked to look at might have a particularly important tone. If you are directed to tone, and have to think about it to provide your answer, it will help your understanding or appreciation of the passage as a whole, for example to realise that it is funny, perhaps, or that it is biased.

◆ In other cases, the language of a particular section is rich or its structure is complex so you will not be confined to one technique: you will be given a choice from a list to do what you feel you can handle best. The list prompts you into thinking about these techniques. If a technique has been listed, it is pretty certain that there will be an example of that technique in the lines you are looking at.

◆ Finally, in some cases there is just so much available to comment on in a section of the passage that you are left free to talk about what to you seems most obvious or most effective.

Lists

There are two kinds of lists:

◆ closed lists

◆ open lists.

Closed Lists
An example of a **closed list** would be:

Example 1

How does the writer's language make clear her annoyance with the newspapers?

You should comment on two of the following techniques:

word choice, imagery, sentence structure, tone.

In this case, there are no other options available: you have to do two from that list.

Open Lists
An example of an **open list** would be:

Example 2

How does the writer's language make clear her annoyance with the newspapers?

You should comment on two of the following:

word choice, imagery, sentence structure, tone, or *any other appropriate technique*.

Here you are being given the opportunity to do *any* two techniques which seem to you to be appropriate. The chances are, though, that the ones which have been listed will be useful to you.

Another example of an **open list** would be:

Example 3

How does the writer's language make clear her annoyance with the newspapers?

You should comment on techniques such as word choice, imagery, sentence structure, tone…

'Such as' means that there are other techniques which are not mentioned but which you could try. The three dots indicate that the list could go on for ever.

The ability to work out how a list can be helpful to you is necessary in the Close Reading paper, but it also has a part to play in the Critical Essay paper, as you will see when you get to that section of the book.

Summary

Make sure that you recognise what you are to do in Analysis questions.

In your answer, are you being asked to refer to:

◆ **named** features?

◆ a **closed list** of features?

◆ an **open list** of features?

◆ 'the writer's **use of language**' and make your own list?

How many features? Is it:

◆ one **or** another?

◆ one **and** another?

◆ one **and/or** another?

◆ more than one?

Word Choice

This is a very simple idea. When you are being asked about word choice you are simply being asked to look at the words and see why the writer has chosen those particular words to describe some thing or some feeling, rather than any other similar words.

A person who is under average weight for his or her height, for example, could be called 'underweight', 'skinny', or 'slim'.

What would be the effect if the writer chose the word 'underweight'?

Probably you could say that the person was being looked at in a clinical, sort of medical way, and being seen as in need of treatment. Perhaps the context of the passage might be a political one, talking about disadvantaged areas where people do not get enough to eat.

If the writer chose to use the word 'skinny', what would be the effect?

The person is being described as thin but in an unattractive way, perhaps suggesting something angular and bony.

If the writer chose 'slim', what would be the effect of this particular word?

Again the person is being described as thin, but in an attractive way, suggesting perhaps a smooth, neat, elegant appearance.

'Underweight', 'thin', 'skinny' and 'slim' all mean roughly the same, but the effect of choosing one of them instead of the other three is quite powerful. What makes the difference is the **connotation** of each word.

Key Words *and* Definitions

You should be aware of the difference between the **denotation** of a word and its **connotation(s)**.

Denotation – The denotation of a word is its basic, plain meaning, if you like. If you are asked an Understanding question about a word or phrase, what you are trying to give as an answer is its **denotation** – its 'meaning'.

Connotation – When you are asked an Analysis question about word choice you are required to give the **connotation(s)** of the word – which contribute to its impact or effect.

To take our present example:

Word	Denotation	Connotation
Underweight	Thin	A clinical, sort of medical picture, being seen as in need of treatment
Skinny	Thin	In an unattractive way, perhaps suggesting something angular, bony
Slim	Thin	In an attractive way, suggesting perhaps a smooth, neat, elegant appearance

If we look at a real example you can see how it works.

All the examples in this section are taken from the article on salsa dancing.

Example 1

Transferring the **sultry sensuality** of a Latin* street dance to Edinburgh on a **wet winter's night** would not appear the easiest of tasks. The rain **batters** the glass roof of the studio, competing in volume with the **merengue**** **blaring** from the sound system. In the background, the castle, lit up, **stares down grandly** against the **foreboding skies**.

* Latin is short for Latin American
** merengue is a form of Venezuelan dance music

 Show how the word choice in these lines helps to point up the contrast described here.   2A

Since you are asked for a *contrast* here, it is certain that you will have to look at two examples of word choice: one for each side of the contrast. All the words in bold type could be used in your answer, but it makes sense to choose two words or phrases which you can see something obvious about.

Answer

'Sultry sensuality' suggests something hot and sexy which is normally associated with warm sunny places in contrast with 'foreboding skies' which suggests something dark and threatening and gloomy or 'wet winter's night' which suggests cold, which is inhibiting to the emotions.

Or

Answer

'The rain batters' suggests an assault on the roof, as if the rain is trying to get in and drown out the dancing in contrast with the 'merengue blaring' which suggests something enjoyable, loud, warm and confident.

(You could also mention that both 'batter' and 'blaring' are a bit overdramatised or exaggerated. Useful words to use in this kind of answer could be 'hyperbole' or 'hyperbolic' – words which have connotations of exaggeration.)

Hints and Tips

Note that word choice may be extended to cover a short phrase, as well as single words, but you have to quote exactly what word or phrase you are going to consider in your answer. You can do this by putting the word or phrase you are going to deal with in inverted commas, or you could underline the relevant words. But you have to show the marker which words or phrases you have chosen. You can't write down something as long as 'the castle, lit up, stares down grandly against the foreboding skies'.

Key Points

It is important to realise that normally you get **no marks** for identifying *interesting* words.

If you wrote down 'sultry sensuality' and 'batters' you would get **no marks**.

If you wrote down 'sultry sensuality' and 'batters' and simply say what the words mean you would get **no marks**.

All the marks that you are going to get will arise from the **connotations** which you discuss.

Example 2

Because of the popularity of partner dancing – as opposed to the lone experience of shuffling one's feet and randomly jerking your arms at a club/family wedding – the BBC has decided to make a celebrity version of Come Dancing the centrepiece of its new Saturday night schedule. Fronted by Bruce Forsyth, the show will feature celebrities testing their salsa skills under the guidance of world champion ballroom dancer Donnie Burns.

? How does the word choice in these lines show that the writer thinks that dancing on one's own as opposed to with a partner is not very satisfying. **2A**

The only part of the paragraph which is about dancing on one's own is the bit in parenthesis (between the dashes). Word choice can refer to one or more words/phrases. How many words are you going to attempt to comment on? There are four obvious choices of *word*: 'lone', 'shuffling', 'randomly', 'jerking'. However, there are only two *marks* available so you either want to do one example very well, or do two quite well.

Answer

'Shuffling' has connotations of clumsy, unskilful movements and suggests that the dancing is not very inspired.

Answer

'Randomly' or 'Randomly jerking' suggests that the movements of the dance have no pattern and are made up of arm movements which are not smooth and elegant, but rough and uncoordinated.

The second of these two answers would have been good enough to gain two marks. The first might just have been worth two marks. By doing both you are making certain of full marks. You could not gain any more marks so to go on and try 'lone' would waste time you will need for other questions.

Common Mistakes

It is not enough just to write down 'shuffling' and 'randomly'. You would get **no marks** for that. The marks are available for the comment you make about their **connotations**.

Here are two examples for you to try.

Example 3

Unlikely as it may at first seem, this is occurring across the country. Against similar winter backdrops people are queuing up to learn to dance. National inhibition is being shed as salsa, merengue and cumbia beats force hips to sway rhythmically and partners to twist complicatedly. French ceroc classes are filling up, street dancing to hip-hop is being used as an exercise class. Even ballroom dancing is enjoying something of a renaissance.

? How does the word choice in this paragraph emphasise how popular dancing has become?

2A

Answer on page 85 ➤

Example 4

Admittedly, Saturday night TV may not reek of Latin glamour. But the new *Dirty Dancing* film, soon to reach UK cinemas, makes up for that. Set in the blistering heat of Cuba, Havana Nights features the sort of drippingly sexy salsa that you really have to be Latin to pull off.

? How does the word choice in these lines create an exotic description of salsa dancing?

2A

Answer on page 85 ➤

Summary

1 Quote the word or phrase exactly. Do not leave it unidentified in a longer piece.

2 Give the connotations of the word/phrase not just its meaning (denotation).

Imagery

This is a little harder to grasp than word choice, but once you have understood the approach to imagery questions then you can apply that approach to all examples.

Common Mistakes

Imagery does not mean 'descriptive writing' of the kind which uses lots of adjectives to describe scenes and settings in a series of 'pictures'. For example, although this passage creates pictures of a scene by choosing accurate descriptive words, it is not 'imagery' as it is meant in the context of the Close Reading Paper.

> Down on the level, its pink walls, and straggling roses, and green-painted rain barrel hidden by a thick dusty planting of spruce and larch, was Fin-me-oot Cottage, where house martins flocked to nest in summer, and small birds found plenteous food on the bird tables when the winter came with frost and snow. There, way-wise deer went in the windy autumn dawns to bite at fallen apples in the little orchard.

Imagery in its *technical* sense is mainly concerned with three 'figures of speech':

◆ simile

◆ metaphor

◆ personification.

Also included in this section are other aspects of imagery that work in slightly different ways:

◆ metonymy

◆ symbolism.

1 Simile

This is the easiest of the figures of speech. You all learned about it in Primary School and you know that it is signified by the use of 'like' or 'as (big) as', for example:

◆ 'The messenger ran **like** the wind.'

◆ 'The poppies were **as** red **as** blood.'

When you are asked in a question to deal with these, what do you do? The question will be about the impact or effect of the image.

Example 1

'the messenger ran like the wind'

It would not be enough to say 'the messenger ran very fast' because this just gives the **meaning** of the phrase and you were asked about its **effect**.

A better start would be:

The image (or the simile) 'the messenger ran like the wind' gives the impression of speed because the wind is fast.

But this is still not really going far enough to explain why the writer chose 'wind'. An even better answer would be:

The image (or the simile) 'the messenger ran like the wind' gives the impression of speed because the wind is seen as a powerful force which reaches great speeds. It might also suggest that the runner was going so fast that he was creating a turbulence like a wind.

What you are doing here is recognising some of the **connotations** of 'wind', not just its **denotation**, exactly as we did in the word choice section (see page 41).

Example 2

'the poppies were as red as blood'

Answer

This simile is effective because it tries to communicate the intensity of the red colour of the poppies. The word 'blood' suggests not just colour, but density, perhaps even shininess, which helps you to picture the richness of the poppies.

Hints and Tips

In both the above examples it helps if you can 'see' the image. Can you see the wind? Can you see the blood? If you were painting them, how would you do it? Would the wind be represented by streaks of light? Would the blood be shiny? It helps if you can see these things in your mind's eye, in your imagination.

It is worth noting that in all examples of imagery there is a wide variety of possible answers – it depends on your experience, your range of connotations and your personal 'pictures'.

Here is an example which is not so visual. Instead, it requires a little bit of intellectual input.

Example 3

Too many tourists are so wedded to their camera that they cease to respond directly to the beauty of the places they visit. They are content to take home a dozen rolls of exposed film instead, **like a bank full of Monopoly money**.

? Show how the simile used here highlights the writer's disapproval of the behaviour of the tourists.

2A

Answer

The simile suggests that the writer disapproves of the tourists' behaviour because although there are so many photographs being brought home, and 'bank' suggests that they are valuable, they are actually of no value, in the same way that Monopoly money has no value outside the game. This shows that the tourists had not valued or appreciated the things they were photographing.

This answer recognises the connotations of 'bank' and the connotations of 'Monopoly money' and links it with the writer's disapproval by adding the last sentence – that is, the *effect of the simile*. It is possible (especially in a 2-mark question) that either 'bank' or 'Monopoly money' would be enough.

Remember that you get no marks for simply identifying the simile.

Here is a still harder example.

Example 4

The Thames marks the edge of things. It is what makes north London north, and south London south. Like a twisty ruler, it measures out the intricate social gradations between the east and west of the city.

? Show how the imagery of these lines helps to develop the statement, 'The Thames marks the edge of things.'

3A

In this question you are not told specifically that you have to deal with simile, but when you look at the lines which follow 'The Thames marks the edge of things', you can see that the next sentence does not contain any imagery: it's just making statements which mean exactly what they say (denotation). But the last sentence begins with 'Like' so you are probably

HOW TO PASS HIGHER ENGLISH

going to be dealing with a simile. If you want to make life easier for yourself, you can change the order of the sentence to make it clearer what the simile is. For example:

'It (the Thames) measures out the intricate social gradations between the east and west of the city like a twisty ruler.'

Answer

This simile highlights the function of the Thames because it describes it as being like a 'twisty ruler'. A ruler is normally straight but the river bends so the ruler has to be bendy too. The idea of 'marks out' is developed by the fact that rulers allow you to measure and mark off different lengths, like different parts of the city, and the 'gradations' suggest that you are measuring different levels, like the different classes of people who live there. Therefore the comparison between the river and the ruler gives more detail to illustrate the original statement about the ideas of social classes/areas.

This question was more difficult because you had to cope with the idea of a *development of thought* achieved by the use of the imagery. In the Understanding section (page 24) you saw how to cope with a development of thought through the content and ideas.

Here are two examples to try for yourself.

Example 5

In eight years of living in London, I've found myself tending again and again to the river for consolation. When things won't go, when depression, like a giant squid, gets one in its grip, the Thames is there to clear one's head, to mooch and mutter by.

Show how effective you find the writer's use of imagery in these lines to convey his feelings.

2A

Answer on page 85 ➤

Example 6

She was particularly shocked by one headline A DOOR WE CAN'T CLOSE. She said, 'It makes me feel like vermin.'

Show how the language of these lines shows how strongly she felt. 2A

Answer on page 85 ➤

Hints *and* Tips

Because this question does not ask specifically for any technique, we have to provide the list of possible techniques. In this case the two most obvious are word choice and imagery (simile). You could place 'shocked' and 'vermin' under the heading of 'word choice'; or you could place 'shocked' as word choice and 'It makes me feel like vermin' as a simile, or you could do one of these at great depth. In this case, because we are doing an exercise on imagery, comment on the simile.

2 Metaphor

A metaphor is probably the most powerful (and magical) device in language. If you can get to grips with this aspect of English, you are home and dry.

Metaphor goes one step further than simile:

◆ Simile says something is **like** something – the woman is like a cat.

◆ Metaphor says something **is** something – the woman is a cat.

The first of these statements can be 'true' – the way the woman moved reminded you of the way a cat moved, sinuously and quietly, perhaps.

The second of these statements is *not* 'true' – the woman is not, *literally*, a cat; she is human. However, it suggests that the attributes of both cat and woman are shared. The attributes, or connotations of 'cat' are things such as aloofness, elegance, claws, beauty, independence, distrust and aggression. These are all reminiscent of a certain kind of cat, which transfers to a certain kind of woman. The metaphor fuses *the concepts* of 'cat' and 'woman' together to make an entirely new

Figure 3.1 Simile or metaphor?

concept. The connotations of 'kitten' would be entirely different and would suggest a totally different sort of woman.

Good metaphors allow a lot of information to be transferred to the reader economically.

Think about this metaphor:

'In the wind the men clung on to the big, black, circular birds of their umbrellas.'

Can you see the two concepts of 'big, black birds' and '(black) umbrellas' are being compared and condensed into a new visual concept suggesting, among other things, that the umbrellas are now animate beings and have a life of their own?

Let's return to an example we used in the simile section.

Example 1

Too many tourists are so wedded to their camera that they cease to respond directly to the beauty of the places they visit. They are content to take home a dozen rolls of exposed film instead, like a bank full of Monopoly money.

(?) **Show how the metaphor highlights the writer's disapproval of the tourists.**

The metaphor in this example is in the word 'wedded'. The tourist is not literally wedded to his camera – he has not stood in front of an official and said 'I do' or anything like that. But when we look at the connotations of 'wedded' we get a whole lot of ideas like a permanent relationship as the result of being married, a close relationship, a dependency, allowing no interest outside the relationship, which has the *effect* of illustrating how completely indispensable the camera is to the tourist.

If instead of 'wedded' the writer had used 'welded' we would have had a different metaphor to deal with because the tourist is not literally 'welded' to his camera (painful idea) but the connotations would suggest that the camera has become an indispensable part of his being as if it had been bonded by heat to his hand, he can't leave it behind, and he is trapped by it.

Key Points

To work with a metaphor you need to:

1   Identify a metaphor. But you get **0 marks** for that on its own.

2   Show how the connotations of the metaphor help to enlarge, or refine, your idea of what is being described (e.g. a woman, an umbrella, a tourist).

3   Show the link between the connotations that you have chosen and the literal (or denotational) meaning of the words used in the metaphor.

NOTE: **Stages 2 and 3 here could easily be reversed – whichever you find easier.**

1   We recognised 'wedded' as a metaphor because it is not 'true' literally.

2   We could talk about the connotations of 'wedded' which give a censorious impression of the tourist and his use, or misuse, of his camera.

3   We have related 'wedded' to the **literal** idea of **being married**.

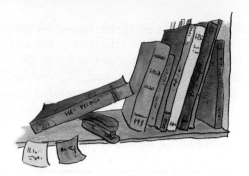

Example 2

The UK is not a group of nations swamped by a tidal wave of immigration. Relatively speaking, Europe contends with a trickle of refugees compared with countries who border areas of famine, desperate poverty, or violent political upheaval.

?   What is the impact of the imagery in these lines in making clear the writer's point?

2A

1	Identify the metaphor(s):	◆ 'swamped' by a 'tidal wave' of immigration ◆ a 'trickle' of refugees. **(0 marks so far.)**
2	Connotations:	The connotations of tidal wave and swamped are to do with a mass of water rushing with unstoppable force onto the land and drowning it as if the number of immigrants is so great that the people of Britain will be overwhelmed and unable to withstand the force of the impact. 'Trickle of refugees' suggests a very small volume of water, having minimal effect on the landscape, like the refugees who are so few in number as to be almost unnoticeable.
3	Link between connotations and literal meaning:	We have related the figurative meaning of 'tidal wave', 'trickle', etc. to their **literal existence as bodies of water**.

Answer

The imagery of 'swamped', 'tidal wave' and 'trickle' help to illustrate the point the writer is making: that in fact there are very few immigrants or refugees. The connotations of tidal wave and swamped are to do with a mass of water rushing with unstoppable force onto the land and drowning it as if the number of immigrants is so great that the people of Britain will be overwhelmed and unable to withstand the force of the impact, which is not true.

By contrast 'trickle of refugees' suggests a very small volume of water, having minimal effect on the landscape, like the refugees who are so few in number as to be almost unnoticeable.

In this question you were not given a specific number of images to deal with. You could have stopped at the tidal wave image and still gained two marks. Equally you could have done 'trickle' and gained two marks. Or 'swamped'. The main reason for doing both here, is that they are, in fact, linked. All three metaphorical ideas are related by their association with water. We call this an **extended image**. When you come across one of these, you can deal with any item alone, or with several together.

Here are some examples for you to try.

Example 3

It would be gravely wrong to try to assess the current state of children's television simply by looking at individual programmes, since they are neither scheduled nor consumed as discrete units. They come as a package, labelled either Children's BBC or Children's ITV, and the glue that keeps the package together is the live continuity links between the shows themselves.

 How does the imagery in these lines help to make interesting points about Children's TV? You should consider two examples. 2A

Answer on page 85 ➤

Example 4

So when Ali did finally refuse the draft, I felt something greater than pride; I felt as though my honour as a black boy had been defended, my honour as a human being. He was the grand knight, after all, the dragon-slayer.

How does the imagery in these lines emphasise the admiration the boy felt for Ali? 2A

Answer on page 86 ➤

Summary

1 Identify or quote the metaphor you are dealing with.

2 Show how the literal and the figurative come together to create an effect.

3 Say what the effect is.

3 Personification

Personification is really just another kind of metaphor. (It's a 'subset', for those who feel mathematically inclined.) In personification some thing or an animal is given human attributes. For example, 'the sky wept' means literally that it is raining, but it is not 'true' (in the sense that a metaphor isn't true), because the sky cannot 'weep' since it has no eyes, tear ducts, nor emotions.

If we were asked to say what the *effect* of 'the sky wept' is, as opposed to 'it was raining', we would find ourselves doing exactly what we did with metaphors (look back at 'wedded'). We look at the connotations of 'wept' and find that we are given a sense of melancholy as if there were something tragic going on under the sky, which required tears to express the sadness.

Key Points

To work with personification, as with metaphor, you need to:

1 Identify the personification. (But you get **0 marks** for that on its own.)

2 Show how the connotations of the personification helped to enlarge, or refine, your idea of what is being described (e.g. the weather).

3 Show the link between the connotations you have chosen and the literal (or denotational) meaning of the personification.

1 Identify the personification: 'the sky wept'. **(0 marks so far.)**

2 Consider the connotations: 'wept' suggests a sense of melancholy, tragedy, tears.

3 Make the link: sadness and melancholy and the literal idea of 'wept' are linked by real rain – as if the universe were in tune with the mood of the description.

Let's consider a more complex example. It's about global warming.

Example 1

Whether the specific storms that scythed down trees in Paris last Christmas, drowned the Po valley last month and battered Britain last week can be attributed to the warming trend is a subject of serious – and contentious – scientific debate.

Show how the writer uses imagery in these lines to emphasise the impact of the storms which affected Europe. You should refer to two examples in your answer.

4A

1   Identify the personifications: 'scythed', 'drowned' and 'battered'. **(0 marks so far.)**

2   Connotations: 'Scythed' gives the impression that the storm was using a scythe to cut down many trees at once as a farmer would use a scythe to cut wheat in one swing. This gives the idea that the storm was incredibly powerful, as trees are infinitely stronger and harder to cut than wheat. It gives a picture of complete devastation.

3   Link between connotations and literal meaning: We have dealt with the literal meaning of 'scythe' by mentioning the farmer cutting down the wheat.

You would now go through the same process with **one** of the other words. Remember, you were asked in this case to consider **two** examples, so there is no point in wasting time on the third one.

Answer

'Drowned' suggests the extreme harm caused to the valley by the water which the storm brought. It is as if the storm had set out deliberately to murder the valley by drowning it. The suggestion is that there was an enormous amount of water flooding the valley.

OR

'Battered' suggests a deliberate assault on Britain by the storm, as if it was literally beating Britain up. It emphasises the extent of the damage caused by the force of the storm.

It is actually not necessary to use the word 'personification'. You could discuss these examples under the general heading of 'Imagery', and there are cases where you might even discuss them under the heading of word choice. As long as you are dealing with the connotations of the words then you will be on the right lines, but to make really sure of the marks with imagery, you have to deal with **both** the **literal** and the **metaphorical** 'meanings'.

Here is another example. (You have already looked at this example under the heading of word choice.)

Example 2

Transferring the sultry sensuality of a Latin street dance to Edinburgh on a wet winter's night would not appear the easiest of tasks. The rain batters the glass roof of the studio, competing in volume with the merengue blaring from the sound system.

Show how the imagery of these lines conveys the reality of a wet night in Edinburgh.

2A

Answer on page 86 ➤

This time you have been asked about imagery, not word choice, so you have to identify the metaphorical usages – in this case, two examples of personification.

Now try this example.

Example 3

And in August this year, a tremor of apprehension ran through the scientific community when the Russian ice-breaker Yamal, on a tourist cruise of the Arctic, muscled its way through the unusually thin ice to the North Pole to find itself sailing serenely into an astonishingly clear blue sea.

? What impression are you given of the progress of the Yamal by the imagery of these lines?

2A

Answer on page 86 ➤

Summary

1 Identify or quote the personification you are dealing with.
2 Show how the literal and the figurative meanings merge to create an effect.
3 Say what the effect is.

4 Metonymy

Metaphor, Simile and Personification work by **comparing** an object with something else and **condensing** two meanings together, for example:

◆ 'the big, black, circular birds of their umbrellas' (metaphor)
◆ 'bats like bits of umbrella' (simile)
◆ 'the umbrellas wept incessantly under a grey sky' (personification).

Metonymy, however, is different. It replaces one object with another which is related to or **associated** with it in some way, for example:

◆ The thing for what's inside it – He was fond of the bottle.
◆ What it's made of for the object itself – The pianist tickled the ivories.

It works by **association**, for example, 'She is addicted to the frying pan' really suggests that she is addicted to fried food. By a process of association, the word 'frying pan' gives access to the whole world of greasy cafés and chip pans.

The substitution of the part for the whole, or the whole for the part – called **synecdoche** – is very like metonymy in the way that it, too, works by **association**. For example: 'a thousand head of cattle' refers not to the severed heads of a thousand cows but to a crowd of beasts, so dense that only the heads are visible and available to count.

An effective article will have a framework:	There will be an overall 'argument':	Typical words/phrases/signposts
◆ a beginning	◆ a question	◆ What are we to gather about this issue?
◆ a middle	◆ a series of points or answers	◆ Firstly/Secondly/Even more crucially…
◆ an end	◆ a conclusion	◆ So, the answer…

OR

An effective article will have a framework:	There will be an overall 'argument':	Typical words/phrases/signposts
◆ a beginning	◆ a proposition	◆ The idea of…is much debated
◆ a middle	◆ a discussion	◆ Some people/On the other hand/But there is also…
◆ an end	◆ a conclusion	◆ On the whole it would appear

There are many other models, which have similar kinds of words and phrases to signal stages in the argument.

These **signposts** or **linking** words/phrases will help you to identify the way the argument of a passage is developing.

There are sometimes questions which ask you to be aware of a detailed kind of structuring signalled by these signposts. For example, if you were asked to show how time was used to structure a section of the passage, and in that section you saw the phrases '**In the past**', '**But now**', '**However, in the future**', you would see immediately that the passage was arranged in a time sequence to clarify the progress of the argument.

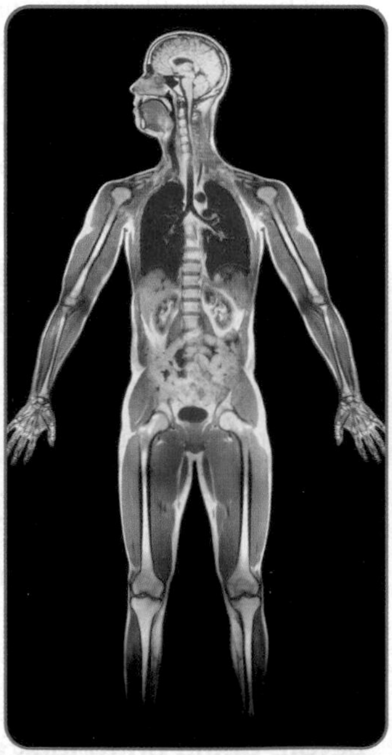

Hints and Tips

Apart from answering individual questions like the one above, the ability to skim quickly through a passage, making use of the **signposts** or **linking words**, can help you enormously in your first reading of a passage, and help you when you come to the questions at the end of the paper, or at the end of an extract. These questions may ask you for an overall impression of what the ideas of the passage are.

Figure 3.2 Linking words are like the joints in a skeleton

Summary

1   First words in paragraphs can act as signposts.
2   The topic sentences of the paragraphs will help you through the argument of the passage. (see page 11)
3   The links between paragraphs (which might be first words or topic sentences) are also helpful. (see page 32)

Sentence Structure

This kind of question seems to present problems to a lot of pupils. Quite often they can see that something is happening because of the way the sentences are structured but they find it difficult to express what is going on.

As with other features, identification is not enough. You need to say what *effect* the feature you have noticed has.

Your comment about sentence structure in relation to Analysis must cover **more than just the meaning**. It must also cover the *effect* of the structure.

One of the keys to success in questions on structure is to remember five main possibilities. Check each of them against the sentences you have been asked to examine.

1a Punctuation

Punctuation is something you should be familiar with. You all know the main punctuation marks in English, and their functions.

Key Points

1   Punctuation and lists
2   Length of sentence
3   Use of climax or anticlimax
4   Repetition
5   Word order

Memorise this list.

Full stop (**.**), comma (**,**), semi-colon (**;**), colon (**:**), exclamation mark (**!**), question mark (**?**).

It is not enough, however, as we have found in the chapters on metaphor and word choice, to identify these features – you have to comment on them.

Hints and Tips

Punctuation as Pointers in a Sentence to Aid Understanding
Punctuation helps the reader to understand what is going on. Full stops tell you when one point has been *finished*. An exclamation mark will give you a clue to the *tone* of the sentence. A colon may signal an *explanation* which you need. Semi-colons may provide you with a *balancing point* in the ideas of a sentence. Brackets, commas or dashes may indicate a *parenthesis*. Inverted commas may cast doubt on the truthfulness of the words they highlight. And so on.

There are Close Reading questions which ask you to show how the punctuation helps to clarify the line of thought in a sentence, often a long sentence.

Here is an example.

Example 1

The panel divided into two teams. One offered a number of alternatives. These included: a 'Landscape of Thorns' – a square mile of randomly-spaced 80ft basalt spikes which jut out of the ground at different angles; 'Menacing Earthworks' – giant mounds surrounding a 2000ft map of the world displaying all the planet's nuclear waste dumps; a 'Black Hole' – a huge slab of black concrete that absorbs so much solar heat that it is impossible to approach.

 Show how the punctuation of the sentence beginning 'These included:' is particularly helpful in following the argument at this stage. 6A

Remember

'Argument' has nothing to do with a quarrel. It is the 'line of thought'.

Answer

The punctuation is helpful in this sentence because it helps to separate out the various solutions. The colon after 'included' shows that there are several solutions coming up. The semi-colons divide up the three solutions (the spikes, the mounds and the slab) so that you can see each solution in isolation. The inverted commas give you the 'name' of each solution as in 'Black Hole' and then the dash after each of the names introduces an explanation of each of the names – a huge black slab.

To be successful in this question you have to know that **one** of the functions of:

◆ a colon is to introduce a list or an explanation
◆ a semi-colon is to divide up long items in a list
◆ inverted commas is to identify titles
◆ a dash is to add information or an explanation.

There are, of course, other functions that these punctuation marks can fulfil.

Here are other examples for you to try:

Example 2

Some argue that the ultimate result of global warming will be a paradoxical but even more catastrophic development: global cooling.

Show how the punctuation clarifies the argument. 2A

Answer on page 86 ➤

Example 3

Governments may stop finger pointing and instead join hands; industries may slash short term profit to permit long term survival.

Show how the punctuation clarifies the argument. 2A

Answer on page 87 ➤

Example 4

Campaigners for drastic cuts in emissions fear that talk of 'adapting' rather than 'mitigating' will ease political pressures on the big polluters such as the US and Japan.

Show how the punctuation helps your understanding. 2A

Answer on page 87 ➤

1b Lists

Numbers of items separated by punctuation marks (often commas and semi-colons) form **lists**.

However, simply mentioning that there is a list is not going to get you very far. As with other features you must also comment on a feature's function and effect.

Example 1

The Scottish race has been variously and plentifully accused of being dour, mean, venal, sly, narrow, slothful, sluttish, nasty, dirty, immoderately drunken, embarrassingly sentimental, masterfully hypocritical, and a blueprint for disaster when eleven of them are together on a football field.

? Comment on the structure and effect of this sentence. 2A

- ◆ Obviously you notice that there are a lot of commas. **(0 marks so far.)**
- ◆ You are aware that the commas contribute to a list structure.
  (Still 0 marks.)

Answer

This sentence consists of a long list of the faults of the Scots. It makes their faults seem endless, as if there were no hope of redeeming features.

This answer comments on the effect of the list on the reader, which is what was asked for.

There are actually other structural comments to make about this sentence. (see page 65)

Example 2

What overwhelms you about this man (Muhammad Ali) from such a violent trade are the goodness, sincerity and generosity that have survived a lifetime of controversy, racial hatred, fundamental religious conversion, criminal financial exploitation, marital upheavals, revilement by many of his own nation and, eventually, the collapse of his own body.

? Show how the writer uses sentence structure to enlist your sympathy for Muhammed Ali. 2A

There are actually two lists here. The first is a short one 'goodness, sincerity and generosity' and the second a much longer one which starts at 'lifetime of controversy' and goes all the way to the end. Let's concentrate on the long one for the moment.

Answer

The list of all the adversities which Muhammed Ali had to face impresses on you what a mountain of difficulties there was piled up against him, so that you sympathise with his situation.

This is quite a satisfactory answer.

Summary

1   Identify the list.
2   Say what effect that list has on the reader.
3   The effect will often be created by the cumulative nature, or the monotony, or the shape of the list.

2 Sentence length

This is easy to spot, but hard to comment on. Generally what you will notice is a short sentence. The passages chosen for Higher English papers will normally have sentences of some length and complexity, so a short simple sentence stands out.

Remember, however, that like all other techniques, you will get no marks for pointing out that there is a short sentence. You have to say what its effect is in the passage.

Here is an example from the Muhammed Ali passage.

Example 1

I used that bat the entire summer and a magical season it was. I was the best hitter in the neighbourhood. Once, I won a game in the last at-bat with a home run, and the boys just crowded round me as if I were a spectacle to behold, as if I were, for one small moment, in this insignificant part of the world, playing this meaningless game, their majestic, golden prince.

But, the bat broke. Some kid used it without my permission. He hit a foul ball and the bat split, the barrel flying away, the splintered handle still in the kid's hands.

? Show how the sentence structure emphasises the impact of the destruction of his bat.

2A

There are a number of quite short sentences in this extract, but there is only one which stands out, begging to be commented on.

Answer

The short sentence 'But, the bat broke' is a dramatic sentence which puts an end to the glory which has been built up surrounding the bat in the previous paragraph. It marks a sudden event which takes the reader by surprise.

You could also point out that its position at the beginning of a paragraph adds to its importance.

The following three examples demand an understanding of any or all of these features –

- ◆ punctuation
- ◆ lists

- ◆ sentence length
- ◆ climax (or anticlimax).

Example 2

Deluges, droughts, fires, landslides, avalanches, gales, tornadoes: is it just our imagination, or is Europe's weather getting worse?

? What is the effect of this sentence as the opening to a passage?

Answer on page 87 ➤

Example 3

Then is a photograph more realistic than a painting? Contrary to the old saying, the camera can lie as easily as the paintbrush – and more effectively, because so many people believe it reproduces reality. It does not. It reproduces appearance, which, as we all know, is quite a different thing.

? How are sentence structure and/or punctuation used here to clarify the argument?

Answer on page 87 ➤

Example 4

Reducing greenhouse gases still won't be enough to prevent severe changes to the world's weather. The scientists' advice to governments, businesses and private citizens about this is grim: get used to it.

? How does the structure of the last sentence in this paragraph highlight the seriousness of the situation?

2A

Answer on page 87 ➤

4 Repetition

This technique is helpful in the analysis of sentence structure, but there are other places where repetition can be seen and its impact analysed.

- ◆ repetition in sentence structure
- ◆ repetition of expressions or words
- ◆ repetition of sounds.

Take one of the more famous statements attributed to Julius Caesar: I came. I saw. I conquered.

Repetition of sentence structure has the effect of suggesting the inevitable move up to the climax of 'conquered'. Repetition of 'I' stresses the importance of the man who did all this, the speed at which he did it, and possibly his egomania.

Example 1

Yet Ireland has managed to attract its young entrepreneurs back to help drive a burgeoning economy. We must try to do likewise. We need immigrants. We cannot grow the necessary skills fast enough to fill the gap sites. We need people with energy and commitment and motivation, three characteristics commonly found among those whose circumstances prompt them to make huge sacrifices to find a new life.

? Show how the writer uses sentence structure to demonstrate her strength of feeling in these lines.

2A

The first thing you should notice is that four of the sentences begin with 'We'.

Next, that two of the sentences begin with 'We need'.

So part of your answer to this question is going to consider the use of repetition as a technique.

Answer

The repetition of 'We' four times and especially two repetitions of 'We need' stress that she feels very strongly about the need for immigration. In a sense she can't say it often enough in the hope of getting through to the reader. (**2 marks**)

And/or

'**And**' is repeated in the list of three qualities which she thinks immigrants provide: 'energy **and** commitment **and** motivation', giving each of these items importance in its own right, having power. (**2 marks**)

And/or

The shortest sentence is 'We need immigrants.' It is deliberately short so that the most important idea in the paragraph is given due emphasis by its separation from the rest and its central position. (**2 marks**)

As you can see, you could identify 'repetition' or 'sentence length' to answer this question. You don't have to do both of them, and the easier one here is repetition, so it's worthwhile looking automatically for any repetition of sentence structure, or phrase, or word in that structure when you are asked to deal with sentence structure.

Example 2

The day that Ali refused the draft, I cried in my room. I cried for him and for myself, for my future and for his, for all our black possibilities.

? Show how the writer's use of sentence structure in these lines helps to convey the passion he felt about Ali's decision. **2A**

Answer

In these sentences there is the repetition of 'I cried' which increases the emotional intensity. The repetition of 'for' phrases – 'for him', 'for myself', 'for my future', 'for his' – deepens the intensity of the emotion still further as it represents gradually the wider importance of his thoughts about Ali's actions. (**2 marks**)

It also builds up to a climax by using repetition (of 'for' phrases) and by combining both his individual and Ali's individual problems into the much more impressive idea of 'all our black possibilities'. (**2 marks**)

Here is an example for you to try.

Example 3

At our end of the time corridor there is a musical cacophony, at theirs a profound and disheartening silence. At our end of the corridor there are a thousand different voices demanding to be heard, demanding our attention… At their cold and gloomy end of the corridor, however, only a trickle of learning or culture survives from classical times, mainly through hearsay and deduction.

? Show how the writer's use of sentence structure makes clear the contrasting environments of the people in the past and the people today. **2A**

Answer on page 87 ➤

5 Word order

Writers play about with word order to create effects. These effects can give more impact to their writing, and stress ideas or feelings which they feel are important. You are probably only going to notice the effects of word order when the order is different from usual. The standard word order in an English sentence is:

Subject	Verb	More information
Jack	ate	a sickening amount of cake that morning.
The Government	is adopting	this measure with enthusiasm.

If you change the word order to make an effect, you could get:

◆ A *sickening* amount of cake Jack ate that morning.

◆ *With great enthusiasm* the Government is adopting this measure.

In each case the sentence is made more vivid and important by putting the interesting feature first: 'sickening', 'with great enthusiasm'.

The same kind of effect can be created by keeping the important word until the end – as you have already noticed with climax or anticlimax.

The chief coach was a strong disciplinarian with his players but **fierce** in the protection of his team.

The chief coach was a strong disciplinarian with his players but, in the protection of his team, **fierce**.

There are other effects of word order but these are the easiest to spot. The beginnings and ends of sentences, paragraphs, lines of poetry, all have the potential to bring something special to the reader's notice.

Summary

1 Punctuation (including lists)
2 Length of sentence
3 Use of climax or anticlimax
4 Repetition
5 Word order

Tone, Mood and Atmosphere

1 Tone

Tone is important in your appreciation of the passages you are given to read. There is nothing worse than reading a passage, taking everything in it very seriously, only to discover later that it was actually tongue-in-cheek, or making fun of the ideas in it.

Unfortunately, in examination situations you are probably feeling so serious about what you are doing that you are not predisposed to find anything funny – but sometimes it is!

It is important to take an **overview** of a passage (see pages 3–4). It's at this stage that it is most useful to recognise an obvious tone. Once you start in on the individual questions you may become very closely focused on the detail of the passage without ever standing back and looking at it as a whole.

HOW TO PASS HIGHER ENGLISH

Considering the Overall Tone of the Passage

Example 1

1   Look at the introduction to the passage.

Passage 1 is taken from film critic Leslie Halliwell's 'The Dead That Walk', his lively history of horror film.

The important word here is 'lively' which suggests that the writing will not be serious but possibly entertaining; and the title 'The Dead That Walk' has a spoof horror feel to it.

2   Look at individual sentences or phrases from the passage:
The mummy films were never a major cycle…but they scared the pants off of plenty of boys of my generation…

This confirms your suspicion that not everything is solemn and serious.

Example 2

1   Look at the introduction to the passage.

Passage 2 is adapted from Lost in Music by Giles Smith. It is 1972 and the author's two older brothers, Simon and Jeremy, take him (at the age of ten) to see the first ever live performance of Relic, the band in which they are drummer and lead guitarist.

You could read this as perfectly straight, but the age of the author, the name of the band, and the idea of the 'first ever live performance' suggest that something might go wrong, and that it might be comic (or tragic).

2   Look at individual sentences or phrases from the passage:
BLAN, BLAN, BLAN, diddle, diddle, diddle…

Again this confirms your opinion that what follows might be comic.

These two hints together should alert you to the fact that it is important for you to recognise the tone. It will not be the normal straightforward informative tone of many of the Higher passages.

You see how helpful it is to read the introductions to the passages (see page 9).

From the introduction and the previous examples you have seen what sort of words can be used to describe 'tone'.

The important concept about tone is the 'voice' that would be used to say the sentence or word.

It would be much easier if someone skilled in reading could be hired to read the passages aloud at the beginning of the exam. You would catch the tone of voice in which various extracts were read. For example: '*Passage 1 is taken from film critic Leslie Halliwell's "The Dead That Walk", his lively history of horror film.*' A good reader would probably read the title, 'The Dead That Walk', in a mock serious tone – a bit over-the-top – and might put imaginary inverted commas round 'lively' so that the word was 'lifted' into your consciousness.

Hints and Tips

Unfortunately this luxury is not allowed in the exam so you have to become a skilled reader yourself. When you come across a tone question try reading the section 'aloud' (but silently!) to yourself – try to hear what the **voice** would do with it. The voice then gives you the tone. And the words we use to describe tone are the same kind of words we use to describe a voice – angry, happy, tongue-in-cheek, serious, humorous, doom-laden, ironic, portentous, hectoring, sarcastic.

When a question specifically asks about tone, you can be pretty sure that there will be a fairly obvious identifiable tone there. The language is unlikely to be just a level, neutral tone.

Because tone is so subjective and individual, there are often many acceptable answers, but the identification of a particular tone is usually only worth something if you *justify your choice* of that tone by referring to the text.

Common Mistakes

It would be too easy to put down 'serious' or 'sarcastic' and just hope that you would be right. You might be, but you won't get any marks until you have given a reason for your choice. Similarly, if you decide to cover all the options and say that the tone seems 'angry, sarcastic and serious' in the hope that one of these choices might be right, you won't get any marks either, even though one of them might be a possible 'correct' answer. This 'scatter-gun' approach does not deceive the marker.

Your answer must contain an identification of an appropriate tone, with a reference to the text to provide evidence for your choice.

Considering Tone in Individual Questions

> ## Example 1
>
> The truth was that he (Ali) was dead scared of flying. Two months earlier, on his way to the U.S. boxing trials, he had been violently buffeted during a turbulent flight across to California. It was the first time he had ever travelled by air and he swore he would never fly again. This was marginally inconvenient when he was one of the hottest hopes America had for Olympic boxing gold.
>
>   'This was marginally inconvenient … boxing gold.'
>
> **?** What tone is adopted by the writer in this sentence? Go on to explain the effect of this tone in the context.   2A

If a skilled reader were reading this aloud, he or she would stress 'marginally' because in fact it was not just **marginally** inconvenient – it was **massively** inconvenient – if he wouldn't fly, he couldn't win! So what tone of voice would the reader use? Many people said the answer was 'sarcastic'. This is always a very popular choice of tone. It's the one most people pick on when they realise that the word doesn't mean exactly what it says. Sometimes they might be right. Often, however, it's not really correct. Sarcasm is usually much more cruel and harsh than the tone is here. Sarcasm is generally when you use one term to mean its opposite. In the example above if the writer had said,

…It was the first time he had ever travelled by air and he swore he would never fly again. **Very heroic behaviour** in one of the hottest hopes America had for Olympic boxing gold.

The tone of 'very heroic behaviour' could properly be described as sarcastic.

So if 'marginally inconvenient' is not sarcastic, what is it? There are a number of possibilities. You could describe the tone as: amused, tongue-in-cheek, humorous, or ironic. There is certainly a smile behind it. The writer finds it mildly amusing, or mildly ironic that this heroic figure, supposedly unafraid, was terrified of flying.

> ## Answer
>
> The tone adopted by the writer here is ironic. He says 'marginally inconvenient' when he in fact means it would be very inconvenient. It makes the sentence amusing as he suggests that it is ironic that the unafraid boxer was scared of flying.

In this answer there is:

◆ the **identification of tone** (usually not enough on its own);

◆ the **evidence**: the words that 'contain' the tone; 'marginally inconvenient' (possibly **1 mark**);

◆ and the comment about its **effect**. (**1 mark** or more).

Example 2

Yet Ireland has managed to attract its young entrepreneurs back to help drive a burgeoning economy. We **must** try to do likewise. We **need** immigrants. We **cannot** grow the necessary skills fast enough to fill the gap sites. We **need** people with energy and commitment and motivation, three characteristics commonly found among those whose circumstances prompt them to make huge sacrifices to find a new life.

? Show how the writer uses tone to demonstrate her strength of feeling in these lines.

2A

You have seen this example before in the section of repetition on page 67 where the question asked about sentence structure.

What tone would a skilled reader be using when reading this extract? The stresses would come on 'must', 'need', 'cannot', 'need'. These are all words which demand some action. So the tone could be described as demanding, or persuasive, or hectoring or even pleading or desperate.

Notice that again there is a lot of repetition in this extract. How does this contribute to tone?

The repetition of 'We' at the beginning of each sentence stresses the verbs which demand action – 'We *need*…', 'We *must*…' (You can use underlining to show how you think the words are said, which helps to show that you understand the tone.) You could also mention the repetition of 'and' and the way that it builds up all the qualities that are needed, again to stress the necessity for doing something, contributing to the pleading or demanding tone.

'The tone the writer uses here is demanding (or pleading). This is shown by the emphasis put on words like "need" and "must"; by the repetition at the beginnings of sentences "*We must*", "*We need*", "*We need*". The tone stresses the writer's strong view that action needs to be taken now. The tone is further developed by the use of 'and' to emphasise the number of good qualities needed to get these off the ground.'

In this answer there is:

◆ the *identification of tone* (usually not enough on its own);

◆ the *evidence*: the words which 'contained' the tone, 'We need', etc. (possibly **1 mark**);

◆ and the comment about how the tone shows *the strength of feeling*. (**1 mark** or more),

The part of the answer about the use of 'and' would not be necessary, but it could be an alternative way to answer the question.

Hints and Tips

These were questions which demanded that you actually *had to* consider tone. There are a number of other questions where tone is in a list of *possible* techniques for you to comment on. As we said before, if 'tone' is in such a list, it is certain that there will be something sensible to say about tone if you can spot it.

Example 3

And we are certainly not **mean**: we may sometimes be **cautious**, for we have long memories of poverty; but we are just as often **generous to a fault**. We are not hypocritical, **at least not very**. We love nothing better than logical argument, so much so that, in Edinburgh at least, we are sometimes accused of *even making love on a metaphysical level*, which may account for the relatively static population.

Show how the language of these lines contributes towards a complex portrait of the Scots. You should consider tone or sentence structure, or word choice.

2A

This is a **closed** list (see page 39). You have to do only **one** of these features.

The tone here is developed by the use of the words in bold. The tone is tongue-in-cheek, self-deprecating, self-critical.

Answer

The tone is a self-deprecating one, showing that the Scots are not content with a simple look at themselves. It is also critical. The use of 'cautious' instead of 'mean' is making meanness sound more respectable, but still admitting that in a way they are mean. Even the generosity is seen as having something false about it. The use of 'at least not very' suggests that the writer knows that the Scots really are hypocritical.

Here is an example for you to try.

Example 4

(*This passage is about the writer William McIlvanney's childhood*)

Given my working class background I was lucky to be in a house where books were part of the practical furniture, not there as ornaments, but to be read and talked about.

Love of reading led naturally, it seemed at the time, to efforts at writing. If books were not the most sought after domestic adjuncts in our housing scheme (depraved orgies of poetry-reading behind closed curtains), the desire to actually write poetry could have been construed as proof of mental aberration. But this was my next move, one I effected without being ostracised by my peers because, perhaps, I was also very good at football. Having successfully undergone my masculine rites of passage in the West of Scotland, I could indulge in a little limp-wristed scribbling.

Look carefully at the sentence beginning, 'If books were…' (line 3).

a) What is the tone of '…books were not the most sought after domestic adjuncts in our housing scheme'? (lines 3–4)   1A

b) Select any feature of sentence structure or word choice in the rest of the sentence which contributes to this tone and explain how it does so.   2A

c) From the rest of the paragraph, quote a word or phrase which maintains the tone and briefly explain how it does so.   3A

Answer on page 87 ➤

2 Mood

Questions on mood have some things in common with questions on tone. The method is the same. There are three necessities. Your answer must contain:

1 an identification of an appropriate mood;
2 evidence from the text to support your choice;
3 a comment on how the mood is created.

Just as in tone you were looking for the 'voice' in which something was said (or read) so in mood you are looking for an 'emotional' dimension which you can identify in the passage you have been referred to.

You have to be able to isolate some words or phrases which suggest this mood (the evidence) and then (depending on the question) you will have to make some further comment on the creation of the mood.

Example 1

Sometimes, later in the evening, one of them will appear downstairs, a pyjamaed stocky ghost lurking on the fringes of our adult evening (scenes from ER or from war-zones are hastily turned off the TV), and say that they are scared. Scared of monsters, scared of wars, scared of you going away, scared of thunder, scared of a rustle outside the bedroom door, scared of don't know what, just scared. And if we say, but there's nothing to worry about, you're safe, there's nothing there, then they reply that they know that: it's inside their heads and they can't make it go away. It's as if the images that flicker against their eyelids night after night are locked into their skulls when they sleep and go on burning there.

? Identify the mood of these lines. By referring to both imagery and sentence structure, show how the writer creates this mood.

4A

The mood is one of fear or terror (on the part of the child) and concern and/or reassurance (on the part of the parent).

In this case, you are told to look for:

◆   at least one image;
◆   sentence structure.

Let's consider only the mood of terror.

Imagery
Possible images would be: 'flicker against their eyelids', 'locked into their skulls', and 'go on burning there'.

Each of these is a metaphor.

Answer

The images of the things the children have seen in films or on TV are constantly running like a film in their heads as if their **eyelids** were a cinema screen; the images are stuck in their minds and can't get out, as if their **skulls** were acting as barriers or doors that the images can't escape from; or that the images are **burning** into their minds causing pain as if a hot brand had been applied to their skin to make a permanent mark.

Any one of these metaphors dealt with in this way would gain 2 marks.

Sentence structure
There is one really obvious sentence, the long one beginning 'Scared of monsters…'

This clearly consists of a list. It also involves a climax.

This sentence contributes to the mood of terror because it lists the enormous number of different things that the child is frightened of, leading up to the climax of the most terrifying one 'just scared'. As the fear is nameless there can be no help for it. This sentence has the effect of not letting the child escape from the constant and painful reminders of the violence she has seen.

3 Atmosphere

Questions on atmosphere have some things in common with questions on tone. The method is the same. There are three necessities. Your answer must contain:

1   identification of an appropriate atmosphere;

2   evidence from the text to support your choice;

3   comment on how the atmosphere is created.

Just as in tone you were looking for the 'voice' in which something was said (or read) so in atmosphere you are looking for some sort of 'involvement of the senses' which you can identify in the passage you have been referred to.

As evidence you have to be able to isolate some words or phrases which suggest this atmosphere and then, depending on the question, you will have to comment further on the creation of the atmosphere.

Example 2

(*This is from a passage on the River Thames*)

Below Westminster, the river belongs to melodrama. At Dockside, just beneath Tower Bridge on the south bank, one can wander among empty warehouses that still smell of cinnamon, where tramps' fires smoulder on the upper floors and the homeless sleep out the day on acrid sacks. It used to be called St Saviour's Dock and was rechristened 'Savoury* Dock' because of the stench of 'Folly Ditch', the open sewer that flowed into it. It is a shadowy forbidding place; it's hard to look into the inert, scummy water of the dock inlet without expecting to see a body there.

*from the word *savour* meaning 'odour'

?   What is the atmosphere created in these lines? Show how the writer creates this atmosphere.   4A

The atmosphere is one of neglect, unpleasantness, decay.

Both the sense of smell and sight are stimulated in these lines.

'Cinnamon', 'fires smoulder', 'acrid', 'Savoury', 'stench', 'sewer' create the atmosphere of decay with strong smells which become progressively more pungent.

The words 'shadowy', 'inert', 'scummy' suggest fading sight or filmy obscure vision.

To add to the gloomy atmosphere the words 'empty', 'forbidding', 'body' have a hollow ring to them where emptiness may even lead to accidental death.

There are obviously lots of options here. You should choose at least two and not more than four words to comment on if you want to be sure of gaining 4 marks. You could do two choices very well, or four quite well and still make your 4 marks.

Summary

It can be helpful to think of these aspects as follows:

Tone is concerned with voice.

Mood is concerned with emotion.

Atmosphere is concerned with the senses.

You will probably be asked questions which require you to:

Name a tone, mood or atmosphere.

Give an example which reflects the tone, mood or atmosphere.

Comment on how your example contributes to the creation of the tone, mood or atmosphere.

Miscellaneous Techniques

The techniques discussed so far operate at a detailed level of text analysis. Word choice, order, imagery and so on 'fine-tune' the writer's message. They express and support the writer's overall intention at the level of fine detail. However, there are other important techniques which have a broader scope. These techniques operate at structural or outline level, so that the writer's overall plan for developing the argument falls into place.

1 Point of view or writer's stance

2 Contrast

3 Use of questions

4 Use of anecdote

5 Use of examples and illustrations

6 Sound

1 Point of View or Writer's Stance

Point of view is the angle from which a writer personally approaches his or her material, how he or she sees it. Writer's stance is more emphatic – you would expect to find quite strong views expressed on the topic. Writer's stance is where the writer **stands** (and from where he or she presumably is not going to budge).

Understanding these concepts can help you with the **overview** of the passages (see page 9) and with the comparison question involving both passages.

Example 1

Passage 1

In the first passage, Neil Ascherson, a distinguished journalist with the Observer *newspaper, considers society's attitude towards old age and old people.*

Passage 2

The second passage is taken from a collection of writing by mature women entitled 'New Ideas for Getting the Most Out of Life'. Here Mary Cooper explains how and why she intends to continue to grow old 'disgracefully'.

As a first step we can identify Ascherson's point of view as that of an observer, describing to us several attitudes to old age. More information about his stance will probably appear in the article. For example, he might be taking a neutral point of view, or a sympathetic stance or a hostile stance. You would have to read on to find out.

The fact that you find a sentence such as: 'The problem here is political will rather than financial capacity' helps you to identify his stance.

In the second passage we can identify Cooper's point view as an insider. As she is old, she is probably going to have a positive point of view towards elderly people.

The phrase: 'thriving, gossiping, defiant sisterhood' shows her point of view.

Having *identified* aspects of the writers' points of view we would then have to go on and show *how* these points of view were made clear, or persuasive, or …

The comparison question in 'Questions on Both Passages' can ask about the writers' differing points of view.

There are also questions which ask specifically about **point of view or stance**.

Example 2

(*This is from a passage on global warming*.)

Governments may stop finger-pointing and instead join hands; industries may slash short term profit to permit long term survival; populations may realise the cost and embrace huge changes to lifestyle. Only an optimist, though, and an uninformed optimist at that, could believe that humankind will succeed in making such radical changes in time to avert bad weather ahead. So the best advice is to get out the umbrellas and hip boots and head for the high ground. Storms are coming; the water is rising. We – and our descendants – will have to learn to live with it.

What is the writer's point of view or stance?

Answer

He is frustrated by governments' and industries' and populations' inability to do anything quickly enough to stop global warming. He maintains this stance quite strongly as is shown in the bitter tone of the last sentence.

In this case, the writer's stance would seem to be the more appropriate description to use. He obviously feels strongly, and the article is designed to make you feel the same way he does – that is, to persuade you.

2 Contrast

Contrast is a technique often used by writers to differentiate between two aspects of an argument, or two views of an issue. It works by *setting two things against each other* and asking the reader to see what the differences are. Its effect is often to clarify a line of thought.

In its broadest form, it's what you can be asked to do at the end of the paper in 'Questions on Both Passages', where you can be asked to 'compare and contrast'. We will look at these kinds of questions later in the section on Evaluation.

Meanwhile, here is a detailed example about contrast.

Example 1

The supreme athlete and unique showman once deemed by Time magazine to be the most instantly recognised human being in the world, struggled up from a settee, tottered across the carpet and embraced me in an enveloping bear-hug. Facially bloated he could speak only in brief, almost unintelligible gasps.

? **By referring to these lines, show how the writer uses contrast to convey his shock at meeting Muhammed Ali years later.** 2A

- The easiest contrast to use here is probably between 'supreme athlete' and any of the words which suggest that physically Ali was weak: 'struggled', 'tottered'.

- Alternatively, you could take 'unique showman' and contrast that with his inability now to communicate or perform well: 'brief almost unintelligible gasps'.

- A third possibility would be to take 'the most instantly recognised' and contrast that with 'facially bloated'.

The writer conveys his shock by contrasting Ali's past physical glory, the description 'supreme athlete' suggesting that every muscle is honed and ready for combat, with the very weak condition he is in now. 'Struggled' and 'tottered' suggest that his muscles will hardly hold him, that he is a ruin of a man compared with what he once was.

You are dealing with this question by analysing the word choice, so you have to:

◆ Quote the words you are discussing (for which you will get **0 marks**).

◆ Comment on the connotations of these words to **clarify the shocking nature** of the contrast.

3 The Use of Questions

The kind of question which everyone seems to be familiar with is the 'rhetorical question'. As a result, almost all questions are identified by candidates as rhetorical questions when many of them are not.

Rhetorical Questions

A rhetorical question is a way of drawing the reader's, or the listener's (because questions are speechmaking devices) attention to a statement or opinion by putting it in the form of a question. The idea is that you will react more to a question. The question acts as a more emphatic and interesting way to convince you to agree actively with a statement rather than to listen passively. It puts pressure on you to agree with the writer or speaker. It doesn't matter whether the expected answer is 'Yes' or 'No'. The important thing is that you are meant to agree.

Example 1

Who would want to live in such a world – especially in some of the regions likely to be hardest hit [by global warming], which happen to include those already the poorest on the planet?

The writer is inviting us to agree with him that nobody would want to live in such a world. The theory is, that if we respond to the question we will be forced to agree **actively**.

However, not all examples are as clear cut as that.

Example 2

At the end of a passage lamenting the fact that in Britain we always have treated, and still do treat, asylum seekers unsympathetically, the passage ends with two questions.

Are we doomed always to stigmatise the stranger? Must compassion only ever be extended after the event?

Are we meant to agree or disagree with the statements behind these questions? If we answer 'Yes' we are taking a pessimistic view of our society. Is that what the writer wants? If we answer 'No' we are being optimistic about the fact that society can change. Is that what the writer wants? There is no way of telling exactly. It will depend on the tone of the whole passage, and on the examples which have been used before building up to these climactic questions.

Common Mistakes

What you **can't** do is write an answer like this!

> These are rhetorical questions to which the expected answer is 'Yes' (or 'No') and they are used to involve us more in the text.

This is **merely identifying** a technique (rhetorical question) but it is not making any valid comment on its **effect in this context**. It is liable, therefore, to gain **0 marks**.

Non-rhetorical Questions

There are other reasons why a writer might use questions.

1   *Using a question provokes an answer*. If you, as a reader, are asked a question, you may have to provide a solution – which means that you have to engage actively with the writer's line of thought. This is often called 'involving the reader'. But it is not enough to stop there, you have to be precise about the effect of the involvement.

An example from the passage above about asylum seeking starts a paragraph with the question: 'But what does real asylum seeking feel like?'

The question has the effect of making the reader try to answer the question, but then to realise that he or she has little information with which to answer it. The writer then provides the answer in the rest of the paragraph. You have been made to recognise your ignorance, therefore you may pay more attention to the facts you are offered to fill in the gap in your knowledge.

2   *A question can create an atmosphere or set up a tone*. In the passage on old age (see page 9) the question is put right at the beginning of the article: 'How am I growing old disgracefully?'

The reader could not possibly know the answer to this question, so it creates curiosity to see what follows. It also sets up a personal relationship between the writer and the reader, as if this were a conversation.

3   Both of these questions also act as openings to set up topics.

Remember

You have to use your initiative when you are working with questions. But there are two things to remember:

1   Not all questions are rhetorical questions.

2   You must comment on the effect *in the context* of being asked a question.

4 Use of Examples and Illustrations

Writers use examples (or illustrations) to help explain difficult points that they are trying to make. Sometimes an abstract idea is given a concrete example so that the reader can more easily grasp what is happening.

Example 1

Some argue that the ultimate result of global warming will be a paradoxical but even more catastrophic development: global cooling. As the Arctic ice cap melts a flow of fresh water into the North Atlantic could disrupt conveyer currents including the Gulf Stream, which is what keeps northern Europe warm. According to Steve Hall, **'One moment we could be basking in a Mediterranean climate and the next icebergs could be floating down the English Channel.'**

This demonstrates the use of example or illustration (the part marked in **bold**) to clarify the scientific point made before it. It explains the hot/cold paradox by giving a concrete example – 'Mediterranean climate' and 'icebergs in the Channel'.

Example 2

The cause is air pollution that pours greenhouse gases such as carbon dioxide and methane into the atmosphere to produce global warming that can alter weather patterns. **Whether the specific storms that scythed down trees in Paris last Christmas, drowned the Po valley last month and battered Britain last week** can be attributed to the warming trend is a subject of serious – and contentious – scientific debate.

This use of example or illustration (the part marked in **bold**) is slightly different. It is used not so much to clarify the point in this case, as to dramatise it, to make it more immediate by giving you a real picture to consider.

5 Use of Anecdote

An anecdote is a small story or incident included in a passage to give another dimension, or another parallel, to the point being made. It functions like an example or illustration but it is different because it is using a *narrative*, not just a description.

Example 1

According to Steve Hall, 'One moment we could be basking in a Mediterranean climate and the next icebergs could be floating down the English Channel.' It would take just one quarter of 1% more fresh water flowing into the North Atlantic from melting Arctic glaciers to bring the northwards flow of the Gulf Stream to a halt.

And in August this year, a tremor of apprehension ran through the scientific community when the Russian ice-breaker Yamal, on a tourist cruise of the Arctic, muscled its way through the unusually thin ice to the North Pole to find itself sailing serenely into an astonishingly clear blue sea. It was the first time the effects of global warming had been seen so far north.

? **In the context of global warming what is the effect of the writer's anecdote about the Yamal?**

2A

Answer

The story about the Yamal brings vividly home to the reader that this event could not have happened if the effects of global warming were not already well established. It backs up Steve Hall's point that the disaster situation is closer than you would think.

6 Sound

This analytical concept is more often associated with poetry, but it also has a part to play in other genres.

Alliteration

Alliteration is possibly the most instantly recognised sound effect. Everybody can spot it. Everybody can name it. And some can even spell it!

It is, however, very difficult to make a really telling comment about it. Yes, it usually draws your attention to a particular phrase, merely because it is a kind of repetition. But it is the sound **quality** which makes the real effect. Is the repeated sound hard or soft, heavy or light? Is the effect depressing, light-hearted, comic?

Rhyme and Rhythm

Rhyme and rhythm have a whole series of functions in poetry, which you will have been taught about with respect to the poems you have studied, but they can occasionally be used in prose – sometimes for comic effect – but they will perform the same kind of function as any of the repetitive uses of language we have discussed.

Summary

You have to look carefully at these questions because you will not come across a large number of them to practise with.

However, the principle remains the same as in all other aspects of Analysis:

Make a statement which answers the question.

Provide evidence from the text to back up your statement.

Make a comment which links your evidence with the statement.

Answers

Example 3 (page 44)

Queuing up	suggests a never-ending line of people anxious not to miss the chance to dance.
Inhibition is being shed	'shed' suggests that inhibitions are being thrown away in a complete abandonment of caution.
Filling up	becoming so popular that they might overflow.
Even	'even' used before ballroom dancing emphasises how far the craze has gone if such an old-fashioned form of dancing has become popular again.
Enjoying a renaissance	suggests the number of people wanting to do ballroom dancing amounts almost to a coming back from the dead of an old-fashioned and out-of-date form of dancing.

Example 4 (page 44)

Reek	suggests the smell of something animal, sweaty, sexy, settings.
Dirty Dancing	suggests the sexual connotations of the dance – that it is connected with sex – like 'dirty talk'.
Blistering heat	the suggestion that the heat is so intense that it makes paint or skin blister.
Cuba	glamorous location.
Drippingly sexy	suggests sweaty/energetic dancing, or some food connotations that, like ice-cream, it is meltingly attractive.

Example 5 (page 48)

The writer conveys his feelings of depression very effectively by comparing his depression to a giant squid. This suggests that something slimy and overwhelming can hold you prisoner in its tentacles so that you can't get free and are smothered by its body in a suction-like grip.

Example 6 (page 48)

She appears to feel very strongly about this headline because vermin suggests that she feels she is in a very lowly place in society, despised by everyone, as if she were dirty and disease-carrying like the rats and mice which people avoid.

Example 3 (page 52)

'Consumed' takes an interesting view of the child's use of TV. It suggests that the child eats up TV programmes as if they were a food, and just as important.

'Package', 'labelled', suggests that someone takes the programmes and makes them into a kind of bundle that can be passed directly to the child who can see at once what is in them.

Answers *continued* ➤

Answers *continued*

'Glue' is used to describe the continuity links, because these are the things that hold the different parts of the programme together, just as objects can be glued together in a parcel otherwise it might fall apart and its impact be lessened.

'Consumed' and 'consumer' are now so much part of our language in the sense of the users of things that we hardly notice that it is an image to do with eating any more; but it gives you a fresh take on the word when you realise its function as a metaphor.

In your answer you could do any two of these four images, **or** you could do 'consumed' and then do all the other three as one extended image, **or** you could do the last three ('package and labelled' together and 'glue' separately) without doing 'consumed' at all.

Example 4 (page 52)

'Grand knight' and 'dragon-slayer' both recall mythical, fairy-tale sort of stories, with great deeds being accomplished by the hero and this shows that the boy regarded him as almost 'out of this world' in his heroism.

Example 2 (page 54)

'Batters' and 'Competing'.
'Batters' suggests that the rain is mounting an assault on the glass roof, as if it might break it, certainly causing a lot of noise. 'Competing' suggests that the noise of the rain almost drowns out the music, as if the rain was in a contest with the music to see which one is more powerful. It gives the idea of the strength and energy of the rain in Europe.

Example 3 (page 55)

The word 'muscled' gives us the idea of the boat making its way through the ice as if it were a human being shouldering its way through the ice by muscle power. It makes it seem forceful and energetic.

Example 1 (page 56)

Using 'suits' instead of the people wearing the suits has the effect of making the people seem impersonal, only interested in figures, only existing in a business world with no private personalities.

Example 2 (page 56)

Using 'wheels' to represent the whole car might suggest that, apart from moving him from place to place, the speed is the real attraction, or that he is so dependent on them that he is incapable of getting around on his own feet and needs to replace them with wheels.

Example 2 (page 61)

In this case, the explanation comes first, then the answer 'global cooling' follows the colon. Part of the effectiveness of using the colon this way is that it saves the really important idea 'global cooling' until the end, so that the contrast has more of a shocking effect on the reader, as it comes as something of a surprise after the talk of the world warming.

Answers *continued* ➤

Answers continued

Example 3 (page 61)

In this case, the semi-colon is not for listing purposes. It is a balancing point in the sentence. The first half of the sentence says that governments might come to their senses. The second half says that industries might do the same. They are parallel statements balanced by the semi-colon. The effect is to put the two developments together, weigh them up and find that both of them are equally welcome.

Example 4 (page 61)

Inverted commas are used here to suggest that there is something doubtful about the substitution of 'adapting', which is weaker, for 'mitigating', which is stronger. That the campaigners have doubts about the use of these terms is shown by putting them in inverted commas. This makes the reader suspicious and likely to examine exactly what is happening.

Example 2 (page 66)

The list of dreadful weather conditions is a good introduction because it suggests the serious nature of the threats by naming so many different kinds of bad weather. The colon leaves you wondering if there is going to be some explanation of these events. What follows is a sort of explanation in the form of a question, because of all these things our weather appears to be getting worse. The question also has the effect of involving the reader in the topic of the passage – by inviting the reader to look for an answer.

Example 3 (page 66)

The first sentence asks a question about the reality of photography. The next sentence provides the answer, which is that many people think it is realistic. The short sentence 'It does not' is very definite in its denial of the answer. It makes it absolutely clear that the writer is sure of his argument. The last sentence says what photography does do, which provides more back up for his definite statement 'It does not'.

Example 4 (page 66)

The colon is used to introduce the explanation about the advice which the scientists are giving everyone. The fact that the word 'grim' is just before the colon leads you to expect something quite harsh after it – a blunt command 'get used to it'. This acts as a climax to the sentence because you have been led to expect something nasty, and what you get is very nasty indeed.

Example 3 (page 68)

The repetition of 'At our end' and 'at theirs' throughout the paragraph helps to divide up the information so that we are very clear about the contrast between the noise on the one hand (people now) and the silence on the other (people in the past).

Example 4 (page 75)

a) Ironic, mocking.

b) 'Depraved orgies' suggests in an exaggerated way that books were bad enough but poetry was even worse in the eyes of the neighbourhood and he is mocking this attitude.

c) 'Limp-wristed' carries on the idea that literature was regarded with suspicion, and thought not to be normal and manly – in this case the writer is slightly mocking himself.

EVALUATION

When you have to evaluate a piece of writing, you have to judge its effectiveness – the extent to which it achieves a particular effect. Concepts like 'How far does it convince, or how much does it achieve?' are part of evaluation.

The **coding** for this skill is **E**.

In the Close Reading Paper there are at least three kinds of evaluation question:

1   **How effective** do you find…? or To what extent is … successful in…? with reference to a particular **technique** like **imagery**, **word choice** or **tone**.

2   **How effective** do you find…? or To what extent is … successful in…? with reference to an **example/illustration**, or **an anecdote** or **a conclusion**.

3   The evaluation of the **merits of both** passages in the Paper which you find in 'Questions on Both Passages'.

1 Effectiveness of a Technique

This type of **Evaluation** question involves **Analysis**.

Example 1

The UK is not a group of nations swamped by a tidal wave of immigration. Relatively speaking, Europe contends with a trickle of refugees compared with countries who border areas of famine, desperate poverty, or violent political upheaval.

?   Discuss how effective you find the writer's use of imagery (or discuss to what extent you find the writer's use of imagery effective) in these lines in making her point clear. You may refer in your answer to one or more examples.   2E

You will recognise this as an example you have seen before on page 51. The question then was slightly different.

'What is the impact of the imagery in these lines in making clear the writer's point?'

These two questions are very similar, and so are the answers.

Our original answer was as follows but there are some additions in bold to cope with the evaluative part of the question.

Answer

The imagery of 'swamped', 'tidal wave' and 'trickle' **are effective in helping** to illustrate the point the writer is making: that in fact there are very few immigrants or refugees. The connotations of tidal wave and swamped are to do with a mass of water rushing with unstoppable force onto the land and drowning it as if the number of immigrants is so great that the people of Britain will be overwhelmed and unable to withstand the force of the impact, which is not true. By contrast 'trickle of refugees' suggests a very small volume of water, having minimal effect on the landscape, like the refuges who are so few in number as to be almost unnoticeable. **The images of 'tidal wave' and 'trickle' are exaggerated enough to convince the reader of the rightness of the writer's point that the UK is not in danger.**

What we have to do in order to demonstrate evaluation is to add the words above in bold.

Be careful – many Evaluation questions involve Analysis. This is because you cannot discuss the effectiveness of an image without first analysing it.

Here is an example for you to try.

Example 2

(From a description of the writer William McIlvanney's childhood.)

Relatives and friends were always dropping in. They brought news of local doings, bizarre attitudes, memorable remarks made under pressure, anecdotes of wild behaviour. Most of it was delivered and received with a calmness that astonished me. I vaguely sensed, early on, the richness they were casually living among, rather as if a traveller should come upon the Incas using pure gold as kitchen utensils.
The substance that would be *Docherty** was beginning to glint for me in the fragments of talk and caught glimpses of living.

*Docherty was the first novel McIlvanney wrote.

By referring closely to one example of imagery from these lines, show to what extent you find the writer's use of this image effective in conveying the special contribution made by his home life to his future career of writing novels.   3E

Answer on page 96 ➤

Hints and Tips

You must:

◆ identify the image you are going to analyse

◆ analyse the image (see pages 49–51)

◆ say how effective you found it in conveying the special contribution… Very effective? Not bad? Not at all effective?

These questions can be coded E. They are sometimes coded A/E, but whatever the coding, when E is asked for, look out for Analysis also.

2 Effectiveness of an Example/Illustration/Anecdote

We have already looked at the use of example/illustration and anecdote in the Analysis section pages 83–84. The code E or A/E will tell you that you have to make a judgement on top of doing your Analysis.

Example

For example, the question on the voyage of the Yamal (see page 83) could easily have been:

In the context of global warming how effective do you find the writer's anecdote about the Yamal?   2E

Answer

The story about the Yamal brings vividly home to the reader that this event could not have happened if the effects of global warming were not already well established. The contrast between 'muscling' and the unexpected serenity of the sea **clearly emphasises the shocking extent of global warming**. It **backs up** Steve Hall's point that the disaster situation is closer than you would think.

The answer is substantially the same except for the added judgement about its effectiveness.

3 Effectiveness of a Conclusion

Although this kind of question can sometimes turn up as an Analysis question, it is more likely to turn up as an Evaluation question. It could be coded **E** or **A/E**.

This kind of question usually takes one of the following forms:

◆ To what extent do you agree that the final paragraph is an effective conclusion?

◆ How effective do you find this illustration as a conclusion to the passage as a whole?

◆ To what extent do you find the lines *x–y* effective as a conclusion to the line of thought?

◆ Explain, with close reference to the writer's word choice, to what extent you find the final six lines fitting as a conclusion to the passage as a whole.

You can see that in several of these questions the 'passage as a whole' is mentioned. This involves you in a quick re-reading, or at least re-thinking task.

As an example here is the full story of the Edinburgh dance classes. It's only 465 words long, so it's about half the length of the passages you will have to deal with in the exam, but it will serve to give an example of how to tackle this kind of 'conclusion' question.

Example

? How effective do you find the final paragraph as a conclusion to the passage as a whole?

BRITAIN SWINGS ITS HIPS TO THE SALSA RHYTHM

Transferring the sultry sensuality of a Latin street dance to Edinburgh on a wet winter's night would not appear the easiest of tasks. The rain batters the glass roof of the studio, competing in volume with the merengue blaring from the sound system. In the background, the castle, lit up, stares down grandly against the foreboding skies.

The 7.15 Latin dance class is full, as was the six o'clock, as is the 8.30. In the reception area of Edinburgh Dancebase, learners, ranging from the middle aged, fresh from work, to students, mill around waiting to dance.

Unlikely as it may at first seem, this is occurring across the country. Against similar winter backdrops people are queuing up to learn to dance. National inhibition is being shed as salsa, merengue and cumbia beats force hips to sway rhythmically and partners to twist complicatedly. French ceroc classes are filling up, street dancing to hip-hop is being used as an exercise class. Even ballroom dancing is enjoying something of a renaissance.

continued ➤

There are six items in this question which you must get straight in your thoughts before you even can start the answer.

1 Which of the two passages did you find more **persuasive**?

The word in bold is important because that word has to appear in your answer, probably more than once. You need to relate your statements about the passages to the idea of how well you have been persuaded.

2 **Justify** your view…

This means that you have to provide evidence which shows why you found Passage 1 more persuasive than Passage 2 or vice versa. You could just say 'I found Passage 1 more persuasive', but you will get no marks for that statement. You have to *justify* that opinion.

3 …by **referring closely** to…

This means that your evidence must be drawn from the words of the passages. You cannot just make general statements about the passages, you must *quote words from* the passage or *refer to incidents or ideas in* the passage as evidence.

4 …to the **style** and/or **ideas**…

Style covers basically all the work you have done on *Analysis*, and there might be other aspects of Analysis which you might not have been asked about specifically. You can now have a quick look to see if you've missed anything which could be described as a persuasive technique. For example, are there any rhetorical questions?

You have been given no helpful list of techniques to use. So you must provide your **own list** of techniques.

This will contain the usual suspects: imagery, word choice and structure (including ideas like climax) and other techniques such as tone, contrast, use of examples, anecdote…

Ideas cover the content and argument of the passages, things you have deduced from your *Understanding* of the passages.

5 …the style **and/or** ideas…

Remember that this gives you an opportunity to do one or the other, or both.

6 of **both** passages.

You must have material in your answer from both passages. Sometimes, because you are so convinced that one passage is

much more persuasive/interesting /informative you spend all your time on the good points of that one and forget to mention the second one. You do not have to deal with each passage equally, but you do have to consider **both** in your answer. If you don't, no matter how brilliant your answer is on one passage, you cannot get top marks.

Here is another question:

Example 2

Which writer's **style**[1] do you **prefer**[2]?

(?) **Justify**[3] your view by **referring**[4] **to both**[5] passages and to **such features as**[6] structure, anecdote, symbolism, imagery, word choice…

This time you must stick to **style** because no other alternative is allowed.

Such features as reminds you that this is an **open** list, which is there to help you; you can talk about any other aspect of style you like.

If you were setting out to answer this question you should take all the help you are offered. The list suggests imagery and word choice. There have probably already been questions directing you to these techniques in both passages. There may also have been some sentence structure questions, but now is the opportunity to look at the overall structure of both passages and see which is more organised/climactic/ convincing. Anecdote and symbolism are not commonly in lists such as these, so it means that there are examples for you to find. Remember the list is meant to help you, not lead you up some blind alley. There are also other aspects of style that you might have been asked about previously in the passages like tone or contrast, which you could also consider.

So you have plenty of material to search for, some of which you have already analysed in your previous answers. You are in a position to write a full answer to this question. You will have plenty of references to the text to back up what you are saying but the references on their own are no use unless you make a comment about their effectiveness.

Here is another question to see if you can highlight all the 5 or 6 important terms in the question.

Example 3

Which passage has given you a clearer understanding of key issues concerning immigration and asylum seeking? You should refer in your answer to the main ideas of both passages.

5E/U

Answer on page 96 ➤

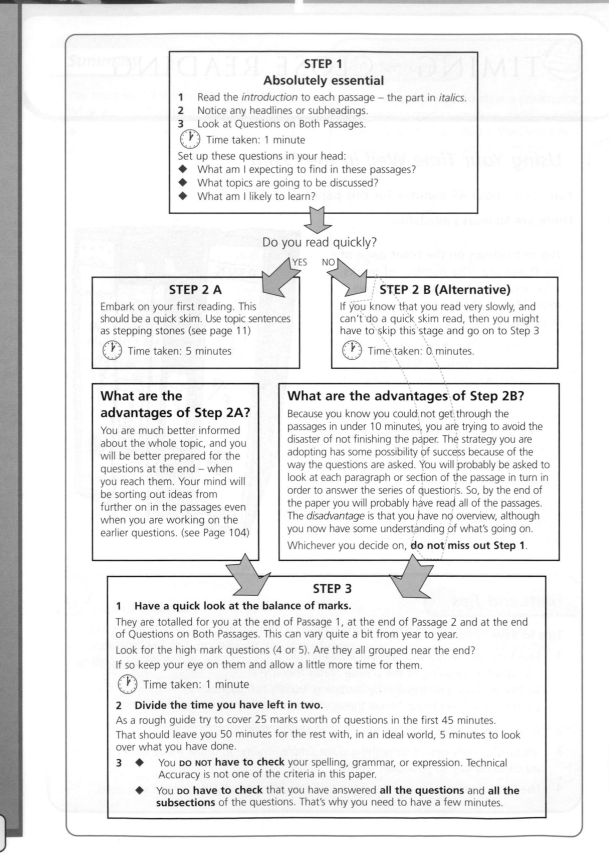

STEP 1
Absolutely essential

1   Read the *introduction* to each passage – the part in *italics*.
2   Notice any headlines or subheadings.
3   Look at Questions on Both Passages.

   Time taken: 1 minute

Set up these questions in your head:
◆   What am I expecting to find in these passages?
◆   What topics are going to be discussed?
◆   What am I likely to learn?

Do you read quickly?

YES   NO

STEP 2 A

Embark on your first reading. This should be a quick skim. Use topic sentences as stepping stones (see page 11)

   Time taken: 5 minutes

STEP 2 B (Alternative)

If you know that you read very slowly, and can't do a quick skim read, then you might have to skip this stage and go on to Step 3

   Time taken: 0 minutes.

What are the advantages of Step 2A?

You are much better informed about the whole topic, and you will be better prepared for the questions at the end – when you reach them. Your mind will be sorting out ideas from further on in the passages even when you are working on the earlier questions. (see Page 104)

What are the advantages of Step 2B?

Because you know you could not get through the passages in under 10 minutes, you are trying to avoid the disaster of not finishing the paper. The strategy you are adopting has some possibility of success because of the way the questions are asked. You will probably be asked to look at each paragraph or section of the passage in turn in order to answer the series of questions. So, by the end of the paper you will probably have read all of the passages. The *disadvantage* is that you have no overview, although you now have some understanding of what's going on.

Whichever you decide on, **do not miss out Step 1**.

STEP 3

1   **Have a quick look at the balance of marks.**

They are totalled for you at the end of Passage 1, at the end of Passage 2 and at the end of Questions on Both Passages. This can vary quite a bit from year to year.

Look for the high mark questions (4 or 5). Are they all grouped near the end?

If so keep your eye on them and allow a little more time for them.

   Time taken: 1 minute

2   **Divide the time you have left in two.**

As a rough guide try to cover 25 marks worth of questions in the first 45 minutes.

That should leave you 50 minutes for the rest with, in an ideal world, 5 minutes to look over what you have done.

3   ◆   You **DO NOT have to check** your spelling, grammar, or expression. Technical Accuracy is not one of the criteria in this paper.

◆   You **DO have to check** that you have answered **all the questions** and **all the subsections** of the questions. That's why you need to have a few minutes.

PART 2

Paper 2: Critical Essay

Critical Skills

The skills of understanding, analysis and evaluation which we have dealt with in the Close Reading paper all have a place in the Critical Essay paper too. If you can analyse a metaphor in a newspaper article, you can do so in a poem.

Writing skills

Writing skills have to be used in this paper because you have to meet a criterion about Expression. Again you have been studying these skills since you were in Primary 3, and in the language unit of your course this year.

Problem solving

Problem solving is the final skill which you have to use in this paper. You are used to this idea in other subjects, but you might not have realised that it is part of the English exam too. You have your content, you have your skills, but you have to apply these in an unknown and unseen environment – the Critical Essay exam. You don't know what question you are going to be asked. You have to wait to find out. Then you have to:

◆ **survey** your knowledge

◆ **select** what you need from your knowledge

◆ then use your **critical skills** to **structure an answer** to the **question you have been asked**.

That is 'solving the problem'.

Common Mistakes

There is no point in trying to second guess what the questions might be – there is an infinite variety of possible questions. There is even less point in writing an all-purpose essay on your text, preparing it, and then using it regardless of the question. The little short cuts which your friends may pass on to you, such as 'Just learn your essay, but make the first paragraph sound as if it's going to answer the question', is fairly suicidal advice. The markers may be tired, it might be after midnight, but they are going to spot that one straight away. By all means practise writing Critical Essays; you have a lot to learn by doing so, but don't assume that you can use any of them again in the exam. The contribution of your essays to your revision plans is dealt with on page 110.

Key Points

The key to this part of the exam is *knowledge* and the *ability to use it flexibly*.

1   You need a good sound body of knowledge about your texts.

2   This process will be dealt with in Mastering Your Text and by using the suggested Study/Revision sheets in Chapter 8 (see pages 114–119).

3   You also have to develop the ability to think rapidly, and shape your knowledge to the questions. The chapters on the individual genres will help you with that. What you have to practise are exercises involving selection and planning.

Becoming Familiar with the Exam Paper

Unlike Paper 1 Close Reading, the Critical Essay paper offers you *choices*. This has advantages and disadvantages.

The advantage is that you are not forced into doing something that you feel unconfident about. For example, nobody can force you to analyse that image about a tortoise which means nothing to you; no one can force you to give an opinion as to which passage is more interesting when you found them both deadly boring.

The disadvantage is that you may:

◆ waste time dithering about which options to choose

◆ not choose the best option for you.

The General Instructions at the beginning of the Exam Paper

1 Answer two questions.

2 Each question must be taken from a different section.

3 Write the number of each question chosen in the margin of your answer booklet.

What You Should Know

You **must** write the number of the question you have chosen, otherwise you are at the mercy of the Marker, who then has to decide which question you are answering, and mark it as if it were that one.

Skills that will be assessed in every answer you write:

4 The relevance of your essay to the question you have chosen, and the extent to which you sustain an appropriate line of thought.

5 Your knowledge and understanding of key elements, central concerns and significant details of the chosen text(s), supported by detailed and relevant evidence.

6 Your understanding, as appropriate to the question chosen, of how relevant aspects of structure/style/language contribute to the meaning/effect/impact of the chosen texts, supported by detailed and relevant evidence.

7 Your evaluation, as appropriate to the question chosen, of the effectiveness of the chosen texts, supported by detailed and relevant evidence.

8 The quality of your written expression and the technical accuracy of your writing.

And all that comes before you have even gone on to read the first question!

Common Mistakes

Chapter 11 develops how you should structure a Critical Essay but it is worthwhile stating here, and probably again later, that there are two ways **not** to structure a Critical Essay.

Unfortunately both ways are quite common, and following them causes many pupils to write a worse Critical Essay than they could.

Do not...

1 Do **not** start your answer by picking two or three techniques from the box at the head of the section and using them as building blocks for your answer. For example, if you pick out character and theme, and then try to answer by dealing with 'character' in isolation and follow that doing the same with 'theme', you will end up repeating yourself and the chances are that the answer to the question will have disappeared down the cracks. It is an even worse approach in poetry because it leads to a fragmented repetitive approach to a poem, looking at 'techniques' individually for their own sake, instead of using them at relevant points in the development of your answer to the question.

Unwise Approach

I am going to show that Macbeth faces a dilemma over whether or not to kill Duncan and that as a result of his decision, he loses the sympathy of the audience. In my answer I am going to consider characterisation and theme.

This is **not** going to provide a line of thought that answers the question. It might answer some of the question in bits and pieces but it has put the techniques first, not the play itself. You should avoid this approach.

2 Do **not** finish your answer with a paragraph dealing with techniques from the box at the head of the section.

Any analysis you use in your answer should come **where it is needed**, not at the end. A remark on sympathy being created by the setting should occur when this has some impact on the discussion about the decision, or the dilemma, or the struggle with conscience – not as an add-on at the end.

CRITICAL ESSAY CRITERIA

Essential Skills

Let's make a list of seven skills you need to be able to show in a Critical Essay. You have to show that you can:

1   understand the main ideas and central concerns of the text
2   sustain a relevant argument, or line of thought
3   engage with the text and evaluate its effectiveness
4   analyse relevant aspects of the writer's craft and identify the impact on the effectiveness of the texts
5   produce evidence to support your line of thought, your analysis and your evaluation
6   write effectively to make your argument clear
7   be technically accurate in your writing.

All of these seven skills are contained in the Performance Criteria for the exam. Because they are all part of the Performance Criteria, it means that you have to 'pass' in each of them. Put another way, if you fail in any **one** of them, you will fail the **whole** essay no matter how good the rest of your skills are. That may seem a bit unfair, but that is what a 'criterion referenced exam' means. You must meet each of the basic criteria to show that you are competent at the level of exam you are sitting.

1 Understanding

This is the basic reading skill. It is being tested in Paper 1 too, but in Paper 2 you are dealing with a text you have been taught and which you should know thoroughly.

At Higher level, you have to understand not just what happens in the text, but be able to see what its central concerns are. The *events* might be about the relationship between a mother and son, but the *central concerns* could be about the stress of the generation gap, or the difficulties (or triumphs) of old age, or the repression of the individual spirit, or any number of things. You could call these themes. A theme, by the way, is not just a single word or idea – 'old age' is not a theme,

but 'the triumphs of old age' could be. Your understanding must include an understanding of the theme(s) of the text. You should also have some insight into the social, psychological, emotional, or philosophical concerns of the text.

2 Relevant Line of Thought

Relevant is a word you are going to come across time and again in talking about this paper. Obviously it means that what you write as a critical essay must be an answer to the question you have been asked and not a complete packaging of everything you know about the text. 'Line of thought' is your answer, your 'argument'. As in a discursive essay, which you might have practised in the language unit of your course, you have to make clear what your answer is, and what the steps in the argument are. A lot will depend on the structure of your essay, which in turn will depend on paragraphing and linkage just as it does in your discursive essay writing.

3 Engagement and Evaluation

Your engagement with the text is shown in your ability to discuss the text, have opinions about it, and ultimately to make a judgement about its success.

4 Relevant Analysis

You have to be able to show how some of the writer's techniques affect the success of the text. They should only be discussed where they are relevant to the particular line of thought you are constructing in your answer. Just putting in a paragraph about word choice because you know something about it is not very useful. What you say about word choice would have to fit naturally into your line of thought, and if it doesn't, don't use it – it is not *relevant* – you will get no credit for it.

5 Evidence

You have to know your text well enough to be able to refer to it in detail as evidence for statements you make in your answer. You will need evidence to:

◆ back up your line of thought

◆ illustrate what you are doing in analysis

◆ support your statements about the success of certain aspects of the text.

References do not always have to be in the form of direct quotations from the text, although sometimes these are necessary. Reference can be made to a particular incident in a novel or play, to prove a point. You will need to learn some quotations, but there is an art to choosing the most useful ones (see pages 164–165).

6 The Quality of your Writing

The quality of your writing, or how fluent your writing is, how good your use of vocabulary is and how well-structured your paragraphs are can make a difference to your mark in two ways.

◆ It is one of the factors which a marker takes into account when reaching a final assessment of your essay. Good use of language should lead to a higher mark.

◆ The more fluent and well-structured your answer, the more you are likely to convince the marker that you really know what you are talking about, and so your mark will be better.

7 Technical Accuracy

This means that your spelling, grammar and punctuation have to be 'sufficiently accurate' to convince the marker that you have the writing skill required for a basic pass in Higher English. You will perhaps remember that the piece of writing you did for your language unit assessment had to be 'consistently accurate'. You had to go away and redraft your work paying due attention to spelling and so on. In the Critical Essay, you cannot go away and redraft your work, and you are doing it under pressure of time. The markers know that, and they may be sympathetic to a few errors due to speed. But they are certainly not going to ignore bad spelling of common words, or the inability to put in full stops where they are required. It follows that you must pay attention to these aspects of your writing – no matter how brilliant your ideas are – and you must leave some time in the exam for checking.

MASTERING YOUR TEXT

How well do you have to know your text? *Very well.*

How do you get to know it very well? *Not by just reading it.*

What do you have to do? *Make organised and sensible study/revision notes in an easily manageable format.*

Your Raw Materials

◆ The text itself – novel, short stories, non-fiction, play, poems, film, TV drama.

◆ Your notes on the text – notes you have taken in class; notes you have been given in class; notes you have made yourself on the text.

◆ Your memory of what was said about the text, what you felt about the text, any discussions you have had about the text.

◆ Any commercially produced notes you have found about the text.

◆ Any essays which you have written about the text.

The most useful of these are: the text, the notes you made on the text, the discussions you had about the text and essays you have written on the text.

Your notes are more useful than the others because they are **yours**. You have had to work at them, you understand what you wrote or said.

Common Mistakes

The trouble with other people's notes is that while you may write them down, you may not understand them or what they can be used for. If you quote them in the wrong context it will show that you don't understand.

If you simply read your text over and over again, no matter how often, you will not be well prepared to answer a question. One thing you can be absolutely sure of is that you will not get a question which asks you to:

'Tell the story of this text'.

If you simply read your text **and** your notes over and over again, you will *still* not be well prepared to answer a question, because you are not going to get a question that asks you to:

'Tell the marker everything you know about this text'.

You have to **organise** the material you have so that you can quickly **select** the areas of your text you need to answer a specific question. (See Chapters 9 and 10.)

Organisation

Gather all the material you have so far (text, notes, essays, etc.) and organise it under different headings or in different 'boxes' so that you know where to find the things you need to answer the question you are given. You will have to select what you need to answer the question, so it helps to know which 'box' you are going to open.

Figure 8.1 Organisation is key

Key Points

To begin with there are basic boxes or headings which will be useful for most genres you might attempt:

- characters
- setting
- themes
- language.
- structure

1 Character
Character covers items you need to know and remember about each important character, for example, their qualities, their motivation, their personalities, their loves and hates and the effect of these on their fate.

2 Themes
Themes will encapsulate the main concerns of the text, for example, the corrosion of jealousy; the power of hysteria; the strength of religious fervour; the struggle between good and evil. Remember that themes are not just one word like 'ambition'; they have to explain what the word does, for example, the 'destructive nature of ambition' or 'ambition rewarded'.

3 Structure
Structure can be large scale: the acts of a play; the turning point of a novel; the climax of a short story. It can also be small scale and used for particular impact: the transition points of a poem; the word order of a line; the repetition of a sound.

4 Setting
Setting can be in place or time. It can involve the customs and morals of a particular society or era. It will inevitably influence the characters and their actions.

5 Language

Language can be concerned with the overall descriptions of a text: a play uses poetic language; a short story may be written in a colloquial style; the general tone of a biography may be adulatory. It can also be concerned with the detailed aspects of language such as word choice, imagery, and all the aspects of language you have studied in the Close Reading paper.

These basic headings need to be subdivided differently in each genre.

At the end of this chapter you will find detailed suggestions about these subdivisions. It is important to start with the **basic** headings. After you are sure about these, you can develop as much detail as you need for your texts as the year goes on.

What You Should Know

By the time you come to look seriously at Chapter 9 Selecting a Question and Chapter 10 Understanding the Question and Selecting Material, you will have to have done some detailed work under each basic heading.

Starting Sorting – 'To begin at the beginning . . .'

Start with the basic 'boxes' or headings. You need a new (large) sheet of paper beside you when you read your text and your notes. On the sheet you start by recording such simple things as the names of the characters – their characteristics, their strengths and weaknesses, for example. But you might do more than that. You might make a division between major and minor characters, or between men and women, or between the Montagues and the Capulets. The way you divide them up will make sense to you.

You might fill your Setting 'box' with a note of where the novel/play takes place. Then setting in time might be important too. There may be more than one theme discussed in your text so you are going to have to have several branches or subdivisions there. Key concerns would be another way of recording these.

If you notice on your way through that one scene is particularly dramatic, or marks a turning point then put that scene somewhere in the Structure area of your page along with other key scenes. (Note the page number so that you can find it again.)

How you organise your material is up to you. You may like to use:

◆ headings and subheadings   ◆ card index

◆ spider diagrams   ◆ tables

◆ family trees   ◆ databases.

Expanding Your Notes

It is important to leave space for your notes to grow.

◆ A card index can grow because you just put more cards in when you need them, and you can rearrange them in different groups if you need to change your mind about something.

◆ A spider diagram or a family tree can be as big as the page you use, or the wall of your room!

- ◆ Headings and subheadings need space like a family tree, to put in more branches as you need them.
- ◆ Tables can be big to start with and subdivided as necessary.
- ◆ Databases are fine, but it's tempting to put in too much – you need to be able to get an overview of what you know.

Look at the examples of these kinds of formats for storing and sorting information on pages 114 and 116–119. There you will find each genre illustrated by a different format.

Hints and Tips

You should choose the style of organisation which suits your mental processes. Are you a list person, or a diagram person?

Once you have decided on a particular form of organisation, you will have to consider the aspects and techniques of the genre which are appropriate for your text. If you decide to use a spider diagram for Drama, for example, it should contain some of the aspects illustrated in the tabulated diagram for Drama on page 116.

Find a method of organisation which makes sense to you and use it for all of your texts.

Look at the following spider diagram showing the possible headings and subheadings which would be helpful to organise the material based on a novel.

The basic boxes are bold outlined. Start with these and work outwards throughout the year as far as you find it useful. You don't have to fill all the boxes!

You have to fill in the details of your text as you learn it. Some of the boxes need to be extended further into details of incident and character. At some point too you are going to have to add quotations. There is an art to choosing quotations (see pages 164–165).

HOW TO PASS HIGHER ENGLISH

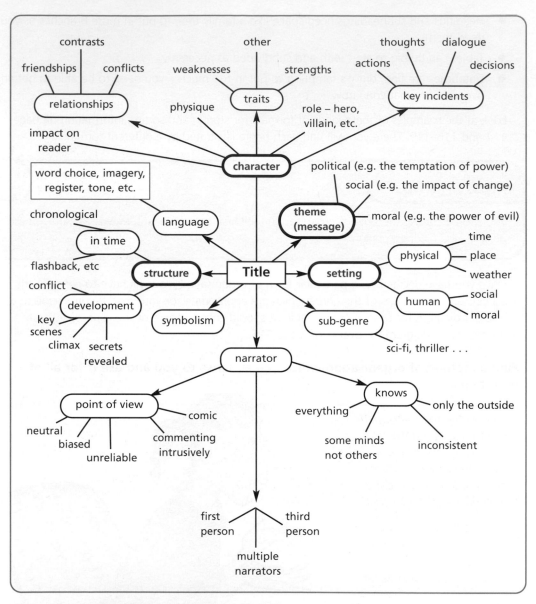

Figure 8.2 Sample diagram for novel or short story

What You Should Know

There is a lot of effort involved in this exercise, but before you go on to consider the **selection of questions** (Chapter 9) or the **selection of material** (Chapter 10) you should organise and complete a study/revision sheet of some kind for each of the texts you are preparing. They may not be complete at this stage, because ideally they should grow with you throughout the year, but the main points should be there if the rest of the advice in this book is to make sense. You have been warned!

Summary

1   Organising your material means you are **actively** engaged in learning. You are not just **passively** reading through the text again!

2   Start at a **simple** level with the basic 'boxes' and **add** only as you develop your understanding of your text throughout the year.

3   What you should end up with is an **organised** set of notes and data about your text.

4   Your data should be in a form which you can **survey** easily and **recall** for your exam.

The samples on pages 116–119 show different suggested ways of organising your material – although there are others that we have mentioned such as index cards and databases not illustrated here. Each of these formats can be adapted to any genre you want to study. You would probably end up with all your notes on Poetry, Novel, Play in the same form – the one that suits you best. All you have to do is transfer the appropriate headings and sections for each genre into your preferred format.

Sample format to assist study/revision (Drama)

Basic Boxes			Evidence	Consequences	Quotation
Theme	political social moral personal				
Characterisation	relationships	conflict contrast friendship			
	traits	strengths weaknesses attitudes motives			
	revealed by	soliloquy aside dialogue actions stage directions			
	role	hero(ine)/catalyst			
	actor input				
Setting	in text	in time in place on stage – how 'real'?			
		social moral			
		stage directions			
		mood			
	in performance	staging lighting sound pace director's input			
Structure	conflict	ideas characters			
	key scenes	origin action consequences impact placing			
(Realistic Absurd Brechtian)	plotting	contrasts (character) contrasts (scene) role/use of character exposition development climax resolution revelation of past			
Audience	participation	4th wall directly addressed in the round narrator			
Language	realism	colloquial heightened poetic (see poetry) use of song			
	style	thematic images metaphor			

Sample family tree (Non-fiction)

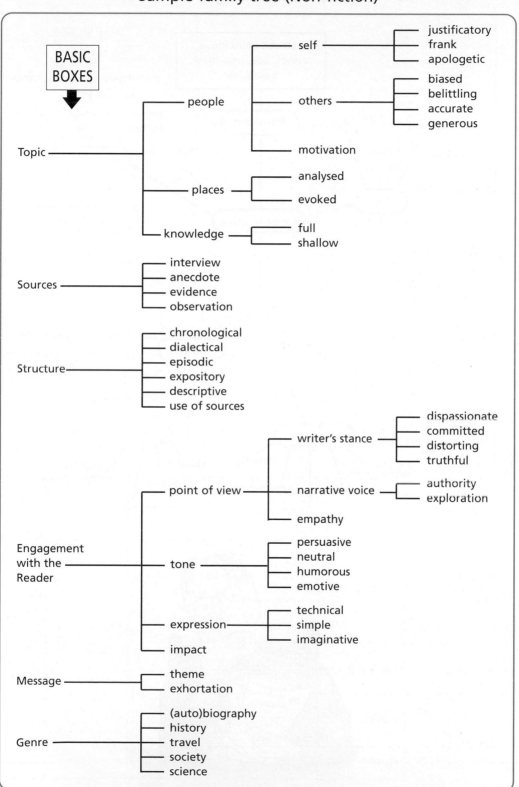

Sample spider diagram (Poetry)

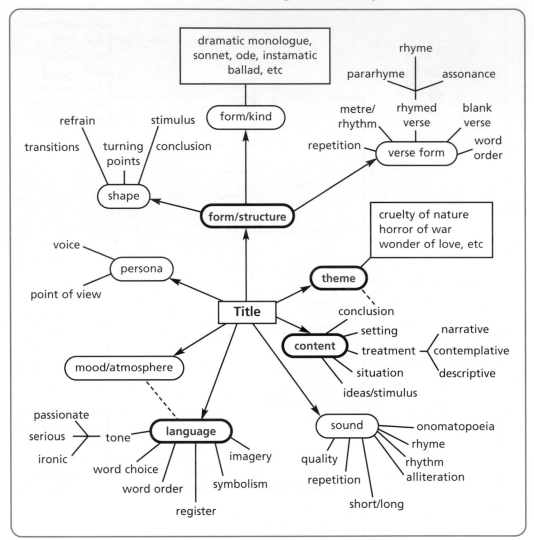

Sample family tree (Film/TV Drama)

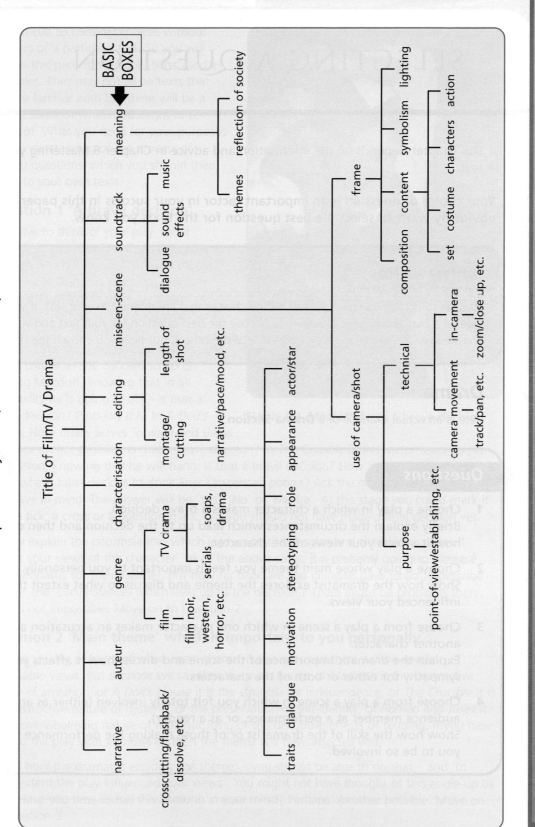

Question 3 A scene involving an 'accusation'

Is there any scene you can identify in a quick run through? Lady Macbeth accuses Macbeth of being a coward. Torwald accuses Nora of bringing his reputation into disrepute. John Proctor accuses Abigail of lying. Tybalt accusing Romeo of being his enemy seems a bit weaker as a possibility.

The 'dramatic importance' of the scene, should be easy to prove in all the above cases. How it affects your sympathy really boils down to 'Whose side are you on?' Another possible choice. But do you know enough about that **one scene**, so that you can use detail from it to open out into the play as a whole? Move on to Question 4.

Question 4 'A scene in which you felt totally involved'

This could be the same scene as the one you picked for Question 3, but here you have a much wider choice – any powerfully dramatic scene will do.

'Show how the skill of the dramatist caused you to be so involved.' In other words, 'What made it dramatic or powerful?' But this presents the same problem as Question 3, even more so. In this answer you should really be writing almost your whole answer based on the **one scene**. Do you know any of the scenes well enough? If you do then it is another possible choice because the question itself is quite easy.

So there you are – four possibilities!

The choice is yours but you have assessed the potential of each question, and haven't missed anything. Nor have you wasted a lot of time, because in your quick running through of the play, you have refreshed your memory and brought facts and ideas up to the surface of your consciousness.

You should now go on to read the other Section or Sections which are going to provide you with your second essay. Remember the advice about reading all the relevant questions before starting your first essay (see page 104).

Poetry

Let's move on to look at the **Poetry** Section.

Questions

1 Choose a poem in which contrast is used in order to clarify a key idea. Examine in detail the poet's use of contrast and show how it was effective in clarifying this key idea.

2 Choose a poet who reflects on the power, the beauty or the threat of the natural world. Referring to one or more poems, show how effectively you think the poet explores her or his main idea(s).

3 Choose a poem which explores one of the following: freedom, friendship, happiness. Discuss to what extent the poem successfully engages your interest in this main idea.

4 Choose a poem which presents a character who provokes you to contempt or anger or irritation. Show how the poet arouses this response from you and discuss how important it is to the overall impact of the poem.

Question 1 'Contrast clarifying a key idea'

You may not have thought of this approach to a poem (unless you have done all the questions from past papers already!) but if you have a quick run-through of your poem(s) in your head, can you identify some contrast(s)? Probably yes. What is the key idea of the poem? This could be something like the theme, or the point the poet really wants to make?

Think about the use of contrast. Can you link it to the way the key idea is expressed? Probably, but you would need to think about it a bit more. So, pass on to Question 2.

Question 2 'The power, the beauty or the threat of the natural world'

This is a **closed** list – no other alternatives are allowed (see page 39).

Obviously this is about the world of nature, the forces of nature, the beauty of nature. Are your poems anything to do with nature in this sense: 'Ode to Autumn', for example, or 'Hawk Roosting', or landscapes, floods and tempests? If not, then you can't do this question. Move on.

Question 3 'Explores one of the following: freedom, friendship, happiness'

This is a **closed** list – no other alternatives are allowed. Perhaps there is some mention of 'friendship' in your poem. Suppose you know

Figure 9.2 A hawk roosting

'Visiting Hour' very well – the poet's friend appears in the poem. Does that make it a poem about friendship? Look at the next part of the question. 'To what extent … in this **main** idea.' Is friendship the main idea of the poem? You have to be able to say 'Yes' **honestly** (not just hopefully) to that question or you are going to find yourself in difficulties. It is not really a suitable question.

Question 4 'Presents a character' who provokes you to 'contempt or anger or irritation'

This is a **closed** list again. It is likely that you would want this character to be the main subject of the poem, otherwise you might not have enough to write about. Show how the poet 'arouses this response' and how important this response (anger or irritation or contempt) is to the overall impact of the poem. Is the feeling about this character important to the overall effect of the poem? If it is, fine.

Because Questions 2, 3 and 4 are closed lists, it is possible that the poem(s) you are thinking of just don't fit – unless you twist them, which is never a satisfactory way to start.

The only one which isn't closed down is Question 1. Go back and think about it. If you know one of your poems well enough it is quite likely that you could have a go at that one, but you would have to **think**.

Prose

If you didn't like the Poetry Section at all, you should, if you're well prepared, have a prose text you could use. So let's look at a **Prose Section**.

In this case, only the first part of the question appears, the part we have called the 'limitation part'. This is a long section, and you can easily discard a number of questions without even having to read the second part, the 'Question itself'.

Questions

1   Choose a **novel** in which a character reaches a crisis point.

2   Choose **two short stories** in which aspects of style contribute significantly to the exploration of theme.

3   Choose a **novel** with an ending which you found unexpected.

4   Choose a **novel** or **short story** in which one of the main characters is not in harmony with her/his society.

5   Choose a work of **non-fiction** which deals with **travel** or **exploration** or **discovery**.

6   Choose a **biography** or **autobiography** in which the life of the subject is presented in an effective and engaging way.

7   Choose an **essay** or a **piece of journalism** which appeals to you because it is both informative and passionate.

- If your prose text is a short story then you can see at a glance that you only have to read Question 2 and Question 4. That is why in this section, and in this section only, the type of text is identified by having it printed in **bold**, so that you won't make mistakes, or waste your time looking at questions which don't concern you.
- If your prose text is a novel there is no point in going past Question 4.
- If your prose text is a non-fiction text then there is no need to read Questions 1–4 at all.

Once you have identified the questions which are relevant to you, you then have to read the second part – the 'question itself' before you can make any decision about whether it is best for you or not.

Hints and Tips

In Question 2 **two** short stories are required. It is not enough to do one story in detail, followed by a very sketchy, half remembered piece on the other. You have to know two short stories well and you will usually be asked to compare or evaluate the two in some way. You should attempt to integrate the discussion of the stories in the essay.

Remember

You are only allowed to do **one** question from each Section, so you can only do one question out of seven in the Prose Section. You cannot do a fiction and a non-fiction text. And you will not get away with using a fiction text for a non-fiction question or vice-versa.

You would follow the same process for selecting questions in the Film and TV Drama Section and the Language Section.

A final warning about choices

If you have not studied carefully and been prepared for answering a question on:

- Non-fiction
- Film and TV Drama
- Language

do not attempt to do these. Do not even look at them.

Find a question from the Sections you have been prepared for: Drama, Novels, Short stories, Poems.

This selection process looks as if it takes a long time, but if you know your texts well enough, the whole process takes less than 5 minutes.

Try this process now with any text(s) you have prepared and organised.

UNDERSTANDING THE QUESTION AND SELECTING MATERIAL

Before we start looking at each of the different genres in turn, there is some common ground which applies to each.

1   You need to have your study/revision materials to hand otherwise you will not be able to benefit fully from the advice.

2   The purpose of these exercises is to take questions and show how you would select the appropriate aspects from your overall knowledge of the texts. Remember that the important part of the question – **the second part** – should provide your line of thought, and therefore your structure for each critical essay.

3   At the top of each Section there is a box containing a number of techniques and features relating to the genre of the Section. The list is an **open** list – you can use any appropriate technique. These suggestions are simply to jog your memory. They might remind you about something (relevant and appropriate) you have forgotten. However, do **not** add a paragraph at the end of your answer about 'symbolism' just because you have suddenly noticed it and do **not** use these features as a method of structuring your essay. (See page 106.)

Drama Section

The purpose of this section is to take one question and show how you would select the appropriate parts from your overall knowledge of a drama text.

Remember

Always keep in mind the fact that a play only exists in its proper sense when it is performed on a stage. Some pupils fall into the trap, half way through their drama answers, of talking about the 'book' as if it were a novel. Although many people write about a play they have not seen performed, they should always attempt to visualise the action while they are reading the text. Stage directions will help, and so will an understanding of the power of theatrical effects, such as soliloquy, the impact of lighting, staging, acting and music.

Figure 10.1 Remember, drama is written to be performed

Question ?

Choose a play whose main theme concerns one of the following: power, corruption, disillusionment.

Explain how the dramatist introduces the theme and discuss to what extent you found the way it is explored in the play enhanced your understanding of the theme.

◆ The list: power, corruption, disillusionment is a **closed** list.

◆ 'Disillusionment' is a word which examiners expect to be part of your vocabulary range. If you are not sure what it means, then you shouldn't attempt to answer a question on the topic of disillusionment in the hope that you have got the meaning right.

Macbeth could be appropriate for the theme concerning power – the misuse of power, or a theme concerning corruption – caused by ambition or power.

Death of a Salesman could be appropriate for the theme of disillusionment with society, or with the American Dream of success.

1 Understanding the Question

The question you have to answer is the second part, the 'question itself':

'Explain how the dramatist introduces the theme and discuss to what extent you found the way it is explored in the play enhanced your understanding of the theme.'

◆ **'introduces the theme'**

This should be quite easy. The information will come from somewhere near the beginning of the play.

◆ **'to what extent'**

This means that you can agree, or disagree, or agree in some areas and disagree in others. Mostly you are probably going to agree, but you don't have to.

◆ **'the way it is explored in the play'**

It will probably be explored through the *characters* in the play, because they are showing you how power or corruption or disillusion happens in the play. It is likely that one of the main characters will be the important point of reference, for example, Macbeth in *Macbeth* (power or corruption), Iago in *Othello* (corruption), Willy Loman in *Death of a Salesman* (disillusion), but other characters can intensify the idea by providing parallels or contrasts with the main exponent of your theme.

The *setting* could also be important in intensifying the impact of the theme, for example, the storms and darkness in *Macbeth*, the urban sprawl suffocating the garden in *Death of a Salesman*. You are covering the skills of understanding and analysis as you go.

◆ **'enhanced your understanding of the play'**

Throughout your discussion of the 'way it is explored' you will be implying or stating that a particular aspect, for example, the setting, added to the effect or atmosphere thus emphasising the theme, making the impact of the theme clearer. So you are evaluating as you go, by showing how the play worked.

Hints *and* Tips

In a question that says: 'To what extent do you sympathise with X?' there is room for a mixture of feelings:

◆ You can agree – I sympathise with X because…

◆ You can disagree – I don't sympathise with X because…

◆ You can do both – sometimes I sympathise with X, sometimes I don't.

Key Words

Useful words and phrases to use when evaluating are 'clearly', 'this very effective scene/speech/image…', 'impressive use of..'.

At this point you might look at the box at the head of the Drama Section:

Answers to questions on drama should address relevantly the central concerns/theme(s) of the text and be supported by reference to appropriate dramatic techniques such as: conflict, characterisation, key scene(s), dialogue, climax, exposition, denouement, structure, plot, setting, aspects of staging (such as lighting, music, stage set, stage directions…), soliloquy, monologue…

You are being reminded about **evidence** ('supported by reference') and **analysis** ('conflict, characterisation, key scene(s) etc.'). In your decision about how to answer this question you have already considered theme, characterisation and setting. It might be that in your study of *Macbeth*, you have looked at symbolism, or imagery which reflect the darkness and depths of the events of the play, so you could use that material as well in your answer.

2 Selecting the Appropriate Material

However, you only have a few minutes to plan this answer. How can you do it quickly?

It goes back to your preparation. If your information is organised in one of the ways suggested on pages 114–119 then you can rapidly **survey** the text in your head, and select what you need to answer this question,

(We are still considering the question on page 127.)

How would you select from your knowledge?

Identify the theme you are going to be considering. Is it introduced by characters? If so, who? And how? Is the theme illustrated through the characters' strengths and weaknesses (revealed by their actions, dialogue, soliloquies)? Is there an important scene which makes clear to you how the characters are dealing with the issues?

Or does setting or atmosphere add to the idea of 'corruption', for example?

What about the effects of theatrical devices, like the staging or music, on your appreciation of the theme?

How does the ending affect you?

You should find that you have selected some areas from your study/revision sheets, but by no means all. This is a good sign. You don't have to show everything you know about the play: you have to use **some** of what you know to **answer the question** you have been asked.

Now try two examples of Drama questions using your study/revision sheets. In each case what you have to do is brainstorm, or highlight the aspects of your information which would be useful for your answer.

Example 1

Choose a play in which a character feels increasingly isolated from the community in which he or she lives.

Show how the dramatist makes you aware of the character's increasing isolation and discuss how it affects your attitude to the character.

Answer on page 146 ➤

Example 2

Choose from a play a scene in which an important truth is revealed.

Briefly explain what the important truth is and assess the significance of its revelation to your understanding of the play.

Answer on page 146–147 ➤

Prose Section – Fiction

The purpose of this section is to take one question and show how you would select the appropriate parts from your overall knowledge of a fiction text.

Question

Choose a novel or short story in which a conflict between two of the main characters is central to the story.

Explain how the conflict arises and go on to discuss in detail how the writer uses it to explore an important theme.

In almost any novel or short story you care to mention there is likely to be a conflict but here the conflict has to be between two main characters – that's probably going to be true of most conflicts (especially in short stories). More importantly, the conflict has to be central to the story.

Take *The Cone Gatherers*. There are several conflicts but Duror versus Callum is certainly important to the story as a whole.

In *Sunset Song* there are several conflicts, but looking for one which is central is more difficult – Chris and her father? Chris and Ewan? The Old Ways and the New Ways? (But that's not a conflict between two characters.) It's not impossible, just a lot more difficult.

Suppose your short story is *The Pedestrian*. There is conflict, certainly, between Mead and the rest of society, but he is the only 'character' mentioned (unless you include the Police Car!) so in this case the task looks (and probably is) impossible.

1 Understanding the Question

The actual question you have to answer is:

> **'Explain how the conflict arises and go on to discuss in detail how the writer uses it to explore an important theme.'**

◆ **'Explain how the conflict arises'** – quite a simple assignment. But don't spend too much time on this as the rest of the question is more important.

◆ **'Discuss in detail'** – you must show real knowledge of the text, specific incidents, character points, key moments which are important for discussing the theme. In this process you will also be engaged in evaluating the text. Useful words and phrases to use when evaluating are 'clearly', 'this very effective description…' and 'impressive use of…'

◆ **'To explore an important theme'** – not just to describe a theme, but to **explore** it – suggests some sort of development of your understanding of the theme.

At this point you might look at the box at the head of the Prose Fiction part of the Prose Section:

> *Answers to questions on prose fiction should address relevantly the central concerns/ theme(s) of the text and be supported by reference to appropriate techniques of prose fiction such as: characterisation, setting, key incident(s), narrative technique, symbolism, structure, climax, plot, atmosphere, dialogue, imagery…*

You are being reminded about **evidence** ('supported by reference') and **analysis** ('characterisation, setting, key incident(s) etc.').

In considering your answer to the question you have already thought about theme, characterisation, key incidents. The idea of development is probably going to bring in structure, and you might like to be reminded of setting. In the *Cone Gatherers* setting probably matters because it is so important to Duror that his forest shouldn't be polluted. (But if it doesn't seem important for your novel or story then don't bother about it, concentrate on the ones that matter.)

2 Selecting the Appropriate Material

However, we're back to this idea that you only have a few minutes to plan this answer. How can you do it quickly? We'll do it as we did the Drama example on page 129.

What would you select?

You would certainly use two main *characters* looking at relationships, contrast, personality traits. Their relationship will be seen in action in key incidents. Obviously you need to identify *theme*. There will be a great deal more information on your sheets (minor themes, for example) which you are not going to use. There may be other aspects which are important for your novel – only you know.

You should find that you have selected some areas from your study/revision material, but by no means all: you have to use **some** of what you know to **answer the question** you have been asked.

Now try two examples of Novel or Short Story questions using your study/revision material. In each case what you have to do is brainstorm, or highlight aspects of your information which would be useful for your answer.

Example 1

? Choose a novel which explores the nature of evil.

Show how the writer's exploration of the theme enhanced your understanding of evil.

Answer on page 147 ➤

Example 2

? Choose a novel which you think has a definite turning point or decisive moment.

Explain briefly what happens at that point or moment and go on to explain why you think it is so important to the rest of the novel.

Answer on page 147 ➤

Prose Section – Non-fiction

Non-fiction covers a huge range of texts, but we can probably evaluate them by considering the:

◆ fullness and fairness of the treatment of the topic
◆ reliability of the material used
◆ effectiveness of the structuring of the material
◆ success of the author's approach to the reader
◆ clarity of the 'message'/themes the author is trying to convey.

The purpose of this section is to take one question and show how you would select the appropriate parts from your overall knowledge of a non-fiction text.

Question

Choose a non-fiction text which made you think about an environmental issue.

Explain briefly what the issue is and at greater length show how the writer's treatment of the issue conveyed her or his point of view.

1 Understanding the Question

The question you have to answer is:

> **'Explain briefly what the issue is and at greater length show how the writer's treatment of the issue conveyed her or his point of view.'**

◆ '**Explain briefly**' – means what it says. You will have a chance to expand on the ideas in the next part of the question.

◆ '**the writer's treatment**' (sometimes this is expressed as the writer's presentation) – means you have to look at how the writer chose, arranged, placed and commented on his material.

◆ '**conveyed her or his point of view**' – was the conclusion clear, were you left in any doubt about the stance the writer took with respect to the issue? How convinced were you?

At this point you might look at the box at the head of the Prose Non-fiction part of the Prose Section:

> *Answers to questions on prose non-fiction should address relevantly the central concerns/theme(s) of the text and be supported by reference to appropriate techniques of prose non-fiction such as: ideas, use of evidence, selection of detail, point of view, stance, setting, anecdote, narrative voice, style, language, structure, organisation of material…*

You are being reminded about **evidence** ('supported by reference') and **analysis** ('ideas, use of evidence, structure, etc.') In considering your answer to the question you have already thought about choice of material and organisation and the writer's stance which gives you his or her point of view. The list reminds you that the use of evidence will be important in backing up the writer's views. And, of course, there are other features that you will probably recall.

Hints and Tips

If you have read the first half of this book dealing with Close Reading, you will find a lot of this material familiar. That is because we are working with non-fiction prose in both, and the techniques and approaches are very similar.

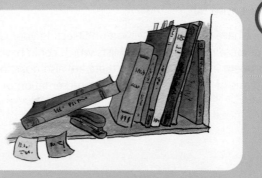

2 Selecting the Appropriate Material

How can you use the few minutes you have to plan this answer? How can you do it quickly?

We'll do it as we did the Drama example on page 129.

What would you select?

You would certainly use issues/theme, point of view or writer's stance, selection of material (evidence, interview, anecdote), and tone (possibly persuasive). With those aspects you probably have enough to write a full and comprehensive answer without anything else.

You should find that you have selected some areas from your study/revision material but by no means all. Again you don't have to show everything you know about the text: you have to use **some** of what you know to **answer the question** you have been asked.

Now try two examples of Non-fiction questions using your study/revision material. In each case you should brainstorm, or highlight aspects of the information which would be useful in your answer.

Example 1

? Choose a biography or autobiography which presented a person's life in an effective way.

Evaluate the techniques the writer uses to make the presentation of the life story effective.

***Answer** on page 147 ➤*

Example 2

? Choose a non-fiction text which introduced you to a new culture.

Explain how effectively the writer's presentation made aspects of that culture clear to you.

***Answer** on page 147 ➤*

Poetry Section

Poetry questions present a slightly different challenge from the other sections we have looked at so far.

As we have seen in the section on Selecting your Question in poetry (see pages 122–124), there are a number of closed lists which could have restricted your choice if you only had one poem in mind. However, there are also questions which ask you to deal with a poem on the basis of its form or structure or presentation of ideas. For example:

- ◆ Choose a poem with an impressive opening.
- ◆ Choose a poem which is written in a specific poetic form, such as dramatic monologue, sonnet, ode, ballad. (Note that this is an **open** list: there are any number of poetic forms like lyric, instamatic, concrete, narrative which you could add to this list to suit your poem or poems.)
- ◆ Choose a poem in which you feel there is a significant moment which reveals the central idea of the poem.
- ◆ Choose a poem in which the poet has created a perfect blend of form and content.

Common Mistakes

Many people choose poetry as one of their texts because poems are shorter than a play or a novel, and so they think poetry must be easier to revise. In fact, some people are very proud of the fact that they have learnt their whole poem off by heart, so the job is done.

1 Merely memorising the whole poem does not mean that you have appreciated it at the level you will need to answer a poetry question.

2 'Their poem' suggests that they have only one poem to call on, which can leave them seriously short of material for the poetry section.

See chapter 12 for how many texts to revise.

Hints and Tips

As mentioned on page 124 there are dangers in trying to make your poem 'fit' into a question which is not right for it. Nature poems, love poems, poems with particular concerns like 'the significance of the past' or 'war or hostility' are quite wide definitions, but perhaps not wide enough to accommodate your poem(s). You have to be sensible and not be tempted into choosing a question which you will have to 'twist' too much.

The other sort of question, the kind which doesn't restrict the subject of your poem (like the ones above), will probably be all right, but you will have to think hard and plan carefully before you write your answer. The following example should help.

Question

Choose a poem in which you feel there is a significant moment which reveals the central idea of the poem.

Show how the poet reveals this in an effective way.

Film and TV Drama Section

This section of the Paper is for **only** those candidates who have studied Film or TV Drama either in class or independently, for Personal Studies, or some other project. You are asked to write a Critical Essay in exactly the same way, and to meet exactly the same criteria, and to display exactly the same skills as in the other genres in the Paper. Your 'reading' of the film involves you in the same processes of understanding and evaluation as the other genres. It requires the same attention to relevance and to the quality of your writing. The only difference will be in analysis, because some of the techniques used to make a film effective are different from those techniques used to make a play or a poem effective. There are other features, of course, which are common to several genres – characterisation, structure, and theme, for example.

In this section there are two types of text specified:

1 Film

2 TV Drama.

TV Drama includes a single play, a series or a serial. This would include, for example, a two-/four-/six-part adaptation of a classic novel, or programmes involving a number of separate episodes, such as *The Bill*, or a continuous narrative such as *EastEnders*.

As in the Prose Section, where both Novels and Short Stories are covered, in the Film and TV Drama Section there may be some questions specifically for Film, some specifically for TV Drama, and there may be some questions which allow both.

You have to check that what you have prepared is allowed for in the question you choose to answer.

To illustrate this, here is the whole of one year's section to see what alternatives are offered.

Questions

1 Choose a film in which one of the characters is corrupted by the society which surrounds him/her.
Briefly describe how the corruption takes hold, and go on to show how the film maker involves you in the fate of the character.

2 Choose a film in which there is a sequence creating a high degree of tension.
Show what techniques are employed to create and sustain the tension in this sequence and how, in the context of the whole film, it adds to your viewing experience.

Questions continued ➤

Questions *continued*

3 Choose a TV drama* which deals with a topical issue in a memorable way. Explain briefly what the issue is and go on to discuss how your interest and emotions were engaged by the treatment of the issue in the TV drama*.

4 Choose a film or TV drama* which makes a major part of its impact through the detailed recreation of a period setting.
Discuss to what extent the setting contributed to your understanding of the concerns of the society depicted in the film or TV drama*.

*TV drama includes a single play, a series or a serial.

There are three questions on film concerning: a character, a sequence and a setting.

There are two questions for TV Drama concerning: an issue and a setting.

It is difficult to look at choices without thinking of a particular text. But with such a wide area as Film and TV Drama it is difficult to imagine one that everyone might have heard of. However, what you need for your purposes is an understanding of the process of picking questions, which you should then relate to your own texts.

Question 1 – **Film only** 'a character is corrupted by the society which surrounds him or her'.

Does your character fit (it could be a main character or a minor character)? Possibly Harry Lime in *The Third Man*, or Michael Corleone in *The Godfather*?

'Briefly describe how the corruption takes hold' will require you to look at some selected parts of the narrative and go on to show how the film maker involves you in the fate of the character. Are you made sympathetic in any way, or is your dislike of the character presented increased as the film progresses? What techniques does the film maker use to keep you interested in the fate of the character? What aspects of *mise-en-scene*, for example?

Question 2 – **Film only** 'a sequence creating a high degree of tension'.

Do you know any sequence in enough detail to answer this question? If you do, go on and look at the next part of the question. 'What techniques are employed to create and sustain the tension'? This requires Analysis of the sequence. But watch for the third part: 'how, in the context of the whole film, it adds to your viewing experience'. This involves you in looking at the structure and theme of the whole film and showing how important this sequence was.

Question 3 – **TV Drama only** 'a topical issue'.

There is a wide choice here, which would suit many of the plays, series or serials you may have studied. Issues such as abortion, poverty, political corruption might appear in the text you have studied. 'Explain briefly what the issue is' means what it says – 'briefly'. The major part of your answer will be on how the 'treatment of the issue' – its presentation involving various techniques of the genre – keeps you emotionally involved and interested.

Question 4 – **TV Drama or Film** 'major impact through the detailed recreation of a period setting'.

Does your text fit this description? *Pride and Prejudice* either as a film or as a TV serial would be an obvious candidate. So would many of the Merchant Ivory films, or *Dr Zhivago*, again as a film or as a TV serial. If your text fits, then look at the rest of the question: 'to what extent the setting contributed to your understanding of the society depicted'. 'To what extent' allows you to say:

◆ the setting was very important to my understanding of the society depicted,

or

◆ the setting, despite making a major impact on me, was not very important to my understanding of the society depicted – there were other factors.

The choice from these four questions is up to you, but you have given each question a fair shot, and haven't missed anything.

Question

Choose a film which has a particularly effective or arresting opening.

Referring in detail to the opening discuss to what extent it provides a successful introduction to the film as a whole.

Note that this question would be appropriate for a large number of films, if you knew the opening in detail.

1 Understanding the Question

The actual question you have to answer is:

> **'Referring in detail to the opening discuss to what extent it provides a successful introduction to the film as a whole.'**

'**Referring in detail to the opening**' – you must have enough evidence that you can 'quote' from the beginning of the film to show how the rest of the film depends on what is there in the beginning.

'**to what extent**' means that you can agree, or disagree, or agree in some areas and disagree in others. You could say that some aspects of the opening are more successful than others in introducing the film as a whole.

'**introduction to the film as a whole**' Is it successful in producing the appropriate mood and atmosphere? What techniques are used to create this mood? Does it introduce characters so that you have an interest in their fate? (characterisation) Does it introduce a theme which becomes important in the course of the film? In discussing these aspects you are showing understanding and analysis as you go. In 'to what extent' and your comments on the success of these aspects of the film you are evaluating also. Useful words and phrases to use when evaluating are 'clearly', 'this very effective use of camera…', 'subtle use of…'.

Now you might look at the box at the head of the Film and TV Drama Section:

Answers to questions on film and TV drama should address relevantly the central concerns/theme(s) of the text and be supported by reference to appropriate techniques of film and TV drama such as: key sequence(s), characterisation, conflict, structure, plot, dialogue, editing/montage, sound/soundtrack, aspects of mise-en-scene (such as lighting, colour, use of camera, costume, props…), mood, setting, casting, exploitation of genre…

You are being reminded about **evidence** ('supported by reference') and **analysis** ('key sequence(s), characterisation, conflict, etc.'). You have already (in your decision about how to answer this question) considered theme and possibly characterisation, and creation of mood or atmosphere, which will probably have involved you in aspects of mise-en-scene and possibly music. Part of the effectiveness will also involve editing, and there may be other features which apply to your film and your opening.

2 Selecting the appropriate material

In common with your other question, you only have a few minutes to plan this answer.

As in the Drama example on page 129, highlight what you would select.

Mise-en-scene (including, perhaps, setting, use of camera and lighting) seems helpful. These techniques could help towards a description of the opening – although there are many other aspects which could be used. You need to mention theme and/or character because there has to be reference to the film as a whole. You might also choose montage (editing perhaps), but obviously the film dictates to you which of these would be best to choose. You can't deal with them all. You have to use **some** of what you know to **answer the question** you have been asked.

Now try two examples of Film/TV Drama questions using your study/revision material. In each case you should brainstorm, or highlight aspects to use in your answer.

Example 1

Choose a film or TV drama in which a particular mood is constructed through key images and elements of soundtrack.

Show how the film or programme makers construct this mood and go on to explain how it influences your appreciation of the text as a whole.

Answer on page 148 ➤

Example 2

Choose a TV Drama with a clear political or social or religious message.

Outline briefly what the 'message' was and go on to explain the methods by which the writer and/or director made you aware of it.

Answer on page 148 ➤

Language Section

This section of the paper is for those candidates who have studied Language either in class or independently, for Personal Studies, or some other project. You are asked to write a Critical Essay in exactly the same way, and to meet exactly the same criteria, and to display exactly the same skills as in the other genres in the paper. Your 'text' is different from the texts of the other genres but you are involved in the same processes of **understanding** and **evaluation**. Your answer requires the same attention to **relevance** and to the **quality** of your writing. There will be differences in **Analysis**, because the concepts dealt with in the study of language are different from those techniques used to make a play or a poem effective. Some of these concepts are more important here than in other genres, for example:

◆ register
◆ jargon
◆ abbreviation
◆ dialect
◆ accent.

But others are more familiar, for example:

◆ tone
◆ word choice
◆ structure.

Your 'text' in Language is the collection of information and examples which illustrate the aspect of language which you have investigated or studied.

This may be spoken or written language, or language transmitted by electronic means. The questions often involve the use of language in different areas or times, in different jobs or professions, in different leisure pursuits and specialities.

Here is the whole of one year's Language section so you can see what alternatives are offered.

Hints and Tips

These questions start with the word 'Consider' and not the word 'Choose' because although you have probably studied several poems and in theory have a choice, you are not expected to have a variety of Language studies at your fingertips. It is assumed that you will be considering the **one** study which you have undertaken. It is likely, then, that only one of the questions in the Language Section will suit your study.

Question

1   Consider the uses of language designed to interest you in a social or commercial or political campaign.
    Identify aspects of language which you feel are intended to influence you and evaluate their success in raising your awareness of the subject of the campaign.

2   Consider the spoken language of a clearly defined group of people.
    Identify features which differentiate this language from standard usage and assess the extent to which these features have useful functions within the group.

3   Consider the language of newspaper reporting on such subjects as fashion, celebrities, reality TV, soap stars…
    Identify some of the characteristics of this language and discuss to what extent it is effective in communicating with its target audience.

4   Consider the language (written and/or symbolic) associated with the use of e-mails or text messaging or instant messaging.
    Describe some of the conventions associated with any one of these and discuss to what extent these conventions lead to more effective communication.

Question 1

'**…social or commercial or political campaign**' covers most areas where persuasive or emotive language is commonly used – charitable appeals, advertisements, political speeches…

'**Identify aspects of language which you feel are intended to influence you**' involves giving examples of emotive/persuasive language in the area you have studied – advertising, for example.

HOW TO PASS HIGHER ENGLISH

list. The conclusions you have reached in your study will give you material for the evaluation aspect of the question. There may also be relevant comments to make about other concepts such as accent or register.

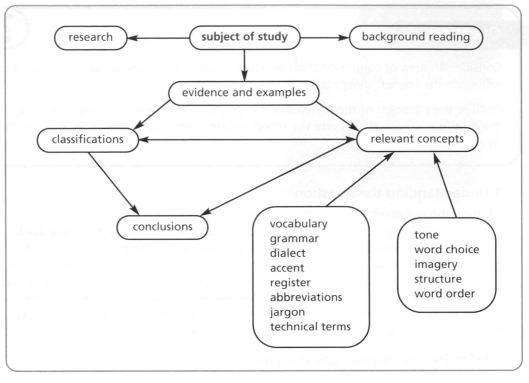

Figure 10.3

Answers

Example 1 (page 129)

You would need the main character – the question focuses on character but a minor character might not give enough material. Personality traits?

Setting and minor characters will be important, since the community from which he or she is isolated is made up of the place and the people. There could also be a breakdown of a relationship with another major character to demonstrate the extent of the isolation.

Key scenes and possibly climax will demonstrate the increasing isolation at various points in the play, so key scenes will be important, and there may be a climactic scene which is even more important.

Example 2 (page 130)

Structure and key scenes – you are being asked to deal with the structure of the play and how the scene involving 'the important truth' fits in with the rest of the play.

Answers continued ➤

Answers *continued*

At least two characters, and probably one of the major characters, will be involved in the revelation of the truth – the importance of the truth cannot be divorced from the characters it affects.

Your understanding of the play will include your appreciation of some of the central concerns of the text, and how the scene relates to these concerns.

Resolution – this is important in your overall understanding of the characters and theme.

Example 1 (page 132)

Theme – the nature of evil – you should not be tempted to deal with any other themes you may have identified in the novel.

The character(s) who embody evil plus those who are affected by it are going to be important in your answer – their relationships, characteristics, morality…

'Exploration' of the theme suggests taking key incidents, which illustrate the working of evil – so structural techniques will be involved – climax, resolution… Setting might also be important to the atmosphere of the novel.

Example 2 (page 132)

Structure and key incident – initially you are being asked to deal with the structure of the novel and how the chosen incident affects the course of the novel.

At least one main character has to be involved for the incident to be so important, and his/her strengths/weakness/relationships will probably be relevant. The importance of the turning point cannot be divorced from the people concerned in it.

A discussion of theme is going to be important to your dealing with the concerns of the novel as a whole and the resolution will be to some extent dependent on the turning point you have identified.

Example 1 (page 134)

The main focus has to be on the person concerned.

Narrative voice and tone may show the writer's attitude to that person.

A chronological structure (if appropriate) and selection of material help to shape the text.

On looking at the box at the head of the non-fiction part of the Prose Section you might notice use of anecdote. This could be part of the presentation of the subject, and that technique might remind you of other aspects – are interviews used, for example?

Example 2 (page 134)

The most obvious aspects of a culture are the place and its people.

Issues encompass the ideas held by the culture, which can be compared with our own society.

Narrative voice and, depending on the text you are dealing with, an aspect of structure.

Answers *continued* ➤

The order you choose will depend entirely on the question you have been asked.

You are not often asked in a question to start at the beginning of your text and go through it in chronological order, commenting as you go, so your structure will have to reflect what is needed.

Here are two examples:

Question

1   Choose a poem in which you feel there is a significant moment which reveals the central idea of the poem,

    Show how the poet achieves this in an effective way.

We have already looked at this example on page 136 but not from this point of view. Where should the starting point be for your essay on this poem?

Begin by looking at the part of the poem which contains the significant moment. It is unlikely to be at the very beginning. Once you have started at 'the moment' you then have to link it to the central concern. That might mean moving forward to explain the significance of the moment, or you might want to go back before 'the moment' and show how the poem develops towards it. Or you might want to do both. It is at this planning/structuring stage that you make these decisions.

Common Mistakes

Do not just begin at the beginning of the poem and work your way through, giving the marker a 'guided tour'.

Question

2   Choose a play in which the conclusion leaves you with mixed emotions but clearly conveys the dramatist's message.

    Briefly explain how the mixed emotions are aroused by the conclusion and then discuss how you are given a clear understanding of the message of the play as a whole.

It is obvious here that you should not start at the beginning of the play. You should start with the conclusion, and its impact on you, before going back into the play to clarify the overall working out of the theme(s) of the play. Notice that the question is helping you to structure your essay. You may not need to go back right to the beginning of the play and work your way up to the end. You should concentrate on the scenes and incidents which are especially important in the development of the theme(s).

Key Points

The important point to note is that the *structure will be dictated by the question* and the text, and may be totally different from any other essay you have already written on that text.

Putting your knowledge into practice using a real text

In the next section we are going to practise.

◆ planning your answer – pages 152–153

◆ writing your essay – pages 154–158.

We are going to use a short story by Lewis Grassic Gibbon entitled 'Smeddum'. Although you probably haven't studied this short story you should be able to follow the principles involved after reading the following synopsis of the story.

Synopsis of 'Smeddum'

The social setting of the tale is a narrow-minded gossipy community which lays strong emphasis on respectability and the bonds of marriage. The narrator relays the censorious attitudes, but knows no more of events than can be seen, heard or related, which makes the climax unexpected.

The physical setting is in the North-east of Scotland, mainly on a poor croft by the sea which is farmed by the Menzies family. The farm is very bleak, wind-swept, and cold. It takes an enormous amount of hard work, mostly Meg's, to make a living out of it. Yet Meg treats her husband, Will, who appears to be a lazy good-for-nothing, with puzzling kindness and is distraught when he dies. Meg is a formidable character, who rules her children with a rod of iron. The oldest boy is made to marry the girl he has made pregnant. She forces her daughter Jeannie's man to marry her, for the same reason. Meg is not particularly popular in the town because she has no fear of class or authority when it comes to protecting her children. With Kath she is freer and more indulgent. When Kath, who has run away with a married man, returns without him after several years to work locally, to the disapproval of the community including her now respectable brother, Meg makes no fuss at all. John Robb has fallen in love with Kath but she refuses to marry him, although she agrees to go to Canada with him. She sends a letter to her mother asking for a loan of money to go there. At the end of the story the family is gathered at the farm on the Sabbath waiting for Kath to come and get her answer. The married ones are appalled by her behaviour and expect Meg to refuse her. At this point Meg tells them that she is going to give Kath the money, because Kath is like her, a strong, free spirit, who has 'smeddum' and doesn't need the conventional bonds of marriage. In a surprise ending she reveals that she was never married to Will.

Question ?

Choose a novel or short story in which a family disagreement plays an important part.

Explain the circumstances of the disagreement and show how the writer uses it to develop your understanding of theme and/or character.

Planning Your Answer (2)

Selection of Content

◆ What the family thinks of Kath

◆ Meg's handling of the rest of her children versus Meg's handling of Kath

◆ Setting in time – social customs, marriage

◆ The 'respectability' of the rest of the family

◆ Theme: the individuality of the rebel; the defeat of conventional 'respectability'

◆ Development of character – Meg – the final piece of the puzzle explaining her attitudes and actions

◆ Key incident: the Sunday when the family meets to see what happens as a result of Kath's letter

Numbering the Content for Structure

◆ What the family thinks of Kath (2)

◆ Meg's handling of the rest of her children versus Meg's handling of Kath (4)

◆ Setting in time – social customs, marriage (3)

◆ The 'respectability' of the rest of the family (6)

◆ Theme: the individuality of the rebel; the defeat of conventional 'respectability' (5)

◆ Development of character – Meg – the final piece of the puzzle explaining her attitudes and actions (7)

◆ Key incident: the Sunday when the family meets to see what happens as a result of Kath's letter. (1)

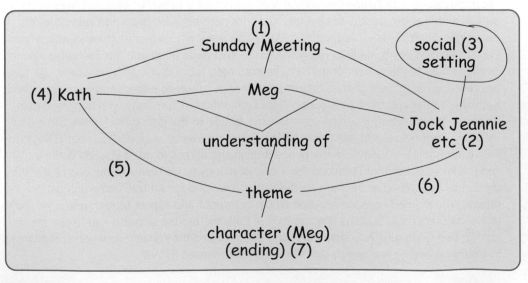

Figure 11.1

This set of notes is much more detailed than yours will be. You can use your own shorthand and scrawls because the only person who has to read it and understand it is you. In this case, for demonstration purposes, everyone has to be able to understand what is going on, so the notes have to be spelt out at a much greater length.

You will see that there are quite a number of aspects of the text which have not been used, for example, setting in place, which in this story, in other questions, could be very important indeed. Similarly, in studying this story, you would have noted aspects of language – imagery and symbolism – but they are not absolutely necessary to answer this question. If you were talking about Kath as a 'free spirit', you might recognise and mention the symbolism of the bicycle in the by-going, which would be something which occurred to you as you wrote your essay, because you know the text so well.

If you manage to cover the ground you have set out in your plan, you will be showing **understanding** of key concerns; in **analysis** you will have dealt with: theme, characterisation, structure (key incident), social setting; and you will have **evaluated** the importance of the incident in the story as a whole, and in your understanding of theme and character. You will have been **relevant** because you have selected from your whole knowledge of the story the bits you need. You will have demonstrated a logical **line of thought** because you have structured your essay sensibly. The last thing you have to do is to check your sentences and spelling to achieve **technical accuracy**.

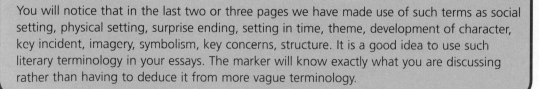

Hints and Tips

You will notice that in the last two or three pages we have made use of such terms as social setting, physical setting, surprise ending, setting in time, theme, development of character, key incident, imagery, symbolism, key concerns, structure. It is a good idea to use such literary terminology in your essays. The marker will know exactly what you are discussing rather than having to deduce it from more vague terminology.

Writing your Essay

In the following section we are going to look at:

◆ opening paragraphs

◆ a paragraph plan

◆ conclusion

◆ how to refer to the writer and his or her craft

◆ the construction of the paragraphs

◆ the use of evidence.

Opening Paragraph

You should always in your opening paragraph tell the marker the *title* of the text, or texts, you are dealing with, and the *name of the author*(s). Make sure you do this accurately – misspelling the name of the author does not make a good opening impression.

You should *refer to the question* – not by slavishly repeating the words of the question but by *indicating, very briefly, the line you intend to take*.

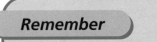

Remember

Put the number of the question in the margin.

For the essay we have been discussing, the opening might be as follows:

> In the short story 'Smeddum' by Lewis Grassic Gibbon the disagreement between the two sides of the Menzies family at the end of the story provides the opportunity to reflect with greater understanding on the character of Meg Menzies, and on the ideas underlying this portrait of unconventional behaviour within a conventional 'respectable' society.

The marker now knows that you intend to focus on an aspect of family disagreement, and show how that relates to the main character's attitude to society.

A Paragraph Plan

In your plan you have noted that number one on your list is the 'key incident' – the Sunday meeting. You need a topic sentence (see pages 11–12) to introduce a paragraph about the incident.

> 1 The family disagreement comes to a head in the final part of the story where the family gathers to await Meg's answer to Kath's letter.

Other topic sentences are needed for each of the steps you have identified in your plan.

2   Grassic Gibbon shows the reader what the 'respectable' members of the family think about Kath.

3   The society in which Grassic Gibbon sets the story is one of a closed rural society where everyone knows everyone else's business and takes a high moral tone with anyone who steps out of line.

4   Meg has always been shown to take Kath's part in family matters and seems to let her do as she wishes as compared with Meg's treatment of the other members of the family whom she forces to conform.

5   . . .

6   . . .

7   The revelation that Meg was never married to Will is kept from us till the very end of the book in order to have maximum impact, and to let us understand many of the unsolved questions raised in the earlier part of the story.

The Conclusion

If your essay hangs together logically, as this one does, then there is no need for any lengthy conclusion. A good conclusion would be made by a statement such as:

> The family confrontation develops our understanding of the narrow moral attitudes of the society in which the story is set and creates a final moment of admiration for the strength of character displayed by Meg.

How to Refer to the Writer and his or her Craft

1 Use of the Writer's Name

When you are referring to the author after the first mention of her or his full name, you use either the surname, or the full name. You do not call the writer only by her or his first name.

You could write:

◆ Lewis Grassic Gibbon creates a character by…

◆ Grassic Gibbon creates a character by…

But not,

◆ Lewis creates a character by…

The Use of Evidence

The previous paragraphs make statements about the story which are illustrated by evidence from the texts both in the form of incident and in the form of quotation. They also contain comment on the evidence to link the evidence to the statements.

For example, in the paragraph about Kath working in the shop we have:

1   Statement: Everyone knows everyone else's business and takes a high moral tone.

2   Evidence: There had been gossip about Kath and the people had protested about her job. (The quotation shows this attitude on the part of the women.)

3   Comment: 'As if they felt they would be contaminated' makes a comment on the stupidity and narrow mindedness of the women. There is the added bonus that the comic quotation makes them seem even more ridiculous.

Hints and Tips

You should notice that the process we have just examined has much in common with a lot of the work we did on Close Reading. You will remember that there the pattern was:

◆   statement

◆   reference to text (evidence)

◆   comment linking the evidence to the statement.

Summary

1   Keep your study/revision material up to date by adding new stuff you have done in class, and revision you have done at home.

2   Practise on as many Critical Essay questions as you can find by using them to:

◆   select the questions suitable to your texts

◆   select the material you need to answer the question

◆   sketch a plan for your answer.

Do this as often as possible to develop speed in your thinking and planning processes. (Don't keep choosing easy questions: look for some where you really have to **think**.)

3   with some of these texts/questions:

◆   write a suitable first paragraph

◆   write topic sentences for your plan

◆   develop some paragraphs to:

    expand your topic sentences, provide relevant evidence, make comment on the evidence

◆   write the concluding paragraph.

This will help to develop speed in your writing.

HOW MANY TEXTS?

This is the big question – one of those FAQs you find when you ask for help on websites.

Common Mistakes

The labour-saving answer is to say 'Two texts because you have to do two questions'.

This is the minimalist approach – and a recipe for disaster unless you are very lucky.

When you worked through the choices in Chapter 9 Selecting a Question, you saw that not all texts you may have studied fit neatly, if at all, into the questions offered in any one year.

Possible Options and their Effects

Three genres studied

If you have studied three genres, then the number of choices you have will start at 12 questions – although, if you have revised both a novel and a short story, you can increase your chances of finding a suitable question in the Prose Section. Although there are only four questions (usually) on fiction, two of them (usually) allow for both a short story and a novel, giving you a better chance of finding a good 'fit' with one of your texts. On the other hand, if you have studied short stories as your prose text, then your choices are probably going to be reduced to two in the Prose Section.

The following table should help to clarify your thinking.

Texts studied	Possible number of questions to choose from	A reasonable 'safe' number of texts
Play(s), novel(s), a selection of poetry.	4 Drama + 4 Novel + 4 Poetry = 12	One play, one novel, several poems
Play(s), short stories, a selection of poetry	4 Drama + 2 Short Story + 4 Poetry = 10	One play, at least two short stories, several poems
Play(s), novel(s), short stories, a selection of poetry	4 Drama + 4 Novel + 2 Short Story + 4 Poetry = 14	One play, one novel and/or short stories*, several poems *If you make a choice of text here, it is probably safer to be the novel.

'Several poems'

How many is 'several'? Well, it's plural so it means at least two, but suggests more. You can be wise in your choice of which poems to revise. You will remember that some of the poetry questions can be 'closed' questions so you want to choose poems which could fulfil a number of functions to spread your options. For example, you could choose two different kinds of poetry – or poems on very different subjects. There is also the possibility that the selection of poems you have studied contains two poems by the same poet, or two poems on the same theme. That might give you the option of doing a 'two poem' question if there were one and it suited you. The most important aspect of the poems you revise is that you should really understand them in depth and that you should feel some real enthusiasm for them.

Two genres studied

If you have studied only two genres, then the number of choices you have will start at 8 questions – although, if you have revised both a novel and a short story, you can increase your chances of finding a suitable question in the Prose Section (see previous page).

The following tables should help to clarify your thinking.

Drama and Prose Texts studied	Possible number of questions to choose from	An absolute minimum number of texts
Play(s), novel(s)	4 Drama + 4 Novel = 8	One play, one novel
Play(s), novel(s), short stories	4 Drama + 4 Novel + 2 Short Story = 10	One play, one novel, one or more short stories
Play(s), short stories	4 Drama + (usually) 2 Short Story = 6	One play, two (or more) short stories

If you revise only one play and one short story you are cutting your options to a dangerous level.

Drama and Poetry Texts studied	Possible number of questions to choose from	An absolute minimum number of texts
Play(s) and a selection of poetry	4 Drama + 4 Poetry* = 8 *Poetry questions sometimes involve **closed** lists, which might cut your options to fewer than 8.	One play and several poems

If you revise only one play and one poem you are cutting your options to a dangerous level.

Prose and Poetry Texts studied	Possible number of questions to choose from	An absolute minimum number of texts
Novel(s) and a selection of poetry	4 Novel + 4 Poetry = 8	One novel and several poems
Novel(s), short stories, selection of poetry	4 Novel + 2 Short Story + 4 Poetry = 10	One novel and/or short stories* and several poems
Short stories and a selection of poetry	2 Short Story + 4 Poetry = 6	Two (or more) short stories and several poems *If you make a choice of text here, it is probably safer to be the novel.

If you revise only one novel and one poem you are cutting your options to a dangerous level.

If you revise only one short story and one poem then you can only be described as having a death wish. With the limitations on the number of short story questions, and the limitations on some poetry questions, you could easily find yourself having to choose two essays from only four questions – not a comfortable situation.

If you have **Film and TV Drama** as one of the genres you have studied, you should regard them in the same light as Prose Fiction – in other words a film is roughly the equivalent of a novel, and TV Drama has the same kind of limitations for choice as the short story.

If you have studied Non-fiction Text(s) you could follow the advice for Prose Fiction, too – but remember, you can only answer **one** question from the Prose section, you cannot answer on fiction **and** non-fiction.

Hints *and* Tips

There is a balance to be struck.

◆   Too many texts may mean that your knowledge is spread too thin.

◆   Too few texts and you could be caught out.

A comfortable number of texts would be:

◆   **two major** texts (full-length plays, novels, autobiographies, films, for example)

and

◆   **two or three shorter** texts (poems, short stories, for example).

If you opt for fewer than that, then you are taking a risk. You might be fine (*if* you're lucky) but you *could have a problem* on your hands if the questions don't 'fit'.

At most you need five study/revision sheets, diagrams, lists – although you might find it difficult to manufacture a fifth wall for the room. (And that's only for English!)

Two Other Options

There are two further categories of texts to mention.

Personal Study Texts

You can use the text for your personal study to answer a question in the exam. After all, it is a play, or a novel, or a film, or some poems, just like the other texts you have studied in your course. You may have invested a good deal of time and effort in it. Is it a good idea to count this as one of your options for revision?

Generally speaking, the answer appears to be 'No'.

There are two reasons for this:

1   You have not had the benefit of actual 'teaching' on this text. You will have had advice on how to tackle your project, but that isn't a substitute for in-depth teaching.

2   You chose your own 'question' you wished to answer for your study. Naturally it would be a question which suited your text and your interests and the way you have seen your text. You will not have had to consider your text from any other angle than your own. Suppose your 'question' was about the effect of the setting on an island in 'Lord of the

Flies'. This provides a good line of thought for your Personal Study, but does it prepare you to answer a question about the dilemma facing the main character?

Language Texts

The most likely reason for attempting a Language question is that you have done a Personal Study which involves investigating some aspect of language. You will have as your 'text' the results of your investigation and, if you have revised your material and your conclusions about the aspect of language you have chosen, you will be well-prepared to answer a question in the Language section.

The second reason for doing a Language question is if you have studied aspect(s) of language in class. You will have notes and examples at your fingertips, and you will understand the concepts behind the studies you have undertaken.

There are no other circumstances in which anyone should attempt a Language question.

Common Mistakes

If you have not studied a film or TV drama in detail, or a non-fiction text, such as a biography, in detail, do not attempt these questions.

We all watch films and TV, and we all read non-fiction from time to time, but that does not prepare us well to write an in-depth answer requiring a knowledge of the techniques of **analysis** necessary to discuss the effectiveness of what we have watched or read.

HOW MANY QUOTATIONS?

As you will have gathered by now, references to the text do not all need to be in the form of quotations. Reference can be made to detailed and specific descriptions or incidents.

However, there are many occasions where a quotation is going to be necessary.

If you want to discuss the mood or atmosphere of the beginning of a novel or short story, it would be helpful to have a quotation which illustrates it.

You can say:

1   Statement: 'A cold bleak setting is created at the beginning of "Smeddum"…' but you can develop the statement by using a quotation to show how the setting is created.

2   Evidence: 'When there wasn't a mist on the cold stone parks, there was more than likely the wheep of the rain…'
    And then you need the third stage of argument which we have been using all the way through this book:

3   Comment: 'The hostile weather and the barrenness of the land show how hard their lives are.'

Choosing Quotations

When you are working on your texts in accordance with the ideas in Chapter 8 Mastering your Text, you are continuously adding to your study/revision material about the text. It is at this stage that you should add some quotations. You need quotations which can illustrate the ideas you have in your 'boxes' – whatever form these boxes take. As you read through a play, there will be certain points at which one of the main characters says something really important to your understanding of the scene – it might be about a decision, or an emotion, or another character. You should make a note of these – that's why you need large sheets of paper or an expandable system. If you are observant you will notice a lot of striking quotations. In other parts of your knowledge chart there will be aspects like themes or issues. They may need a quotation or two as well. So might setting, as we've seen above, or a quotation marking the climax of the play, or the resolution.

What You Should Know

There will eventually be too many quotations for you to learn and remember, but that doesn't matter. You have been *actively engaged* with your texts, you have learned more about them and you have the raw material to start slimming down the number of quotations. There are three ways of doing this:

1   You may find places where one quotation can do two jobs: make a point about a character, and mark a climax in the play – so that's an efficient use of material.

2   You can sift through all the possibles to find the most important, so that instead of six quotations for Macbeth's ambition, you may end up with three.

3   You can shorten the quotations you have chosen down to the bare essentials. It is better to have a number of well-chosen short quotations than two or three long ones. For example, the quotation used earlier about the setting in 'Smeddum' could be shortened to 'the cold stone parks' – it would still provide evidence and allow you to relate the setting to the characters' plight.

There is an exception to this advice when we come to poetry.

You will not be able to rely a great deal on description of incidents and events in poetry (although that is important too). You will probably be engaged in a detailed look at the actual words of the poem. To make a point about the poet's strengths, you might need to quote a slightly longer extract, for example, if an image runs over a few lines. On the other hand, poems are not as long as novels or plays, so that you should be able to remember proportionately more of the text. Some people prefer to learn a whole poem mechanically. They no doubt feel very virtuous and reckon that they could quote from anywhere in the poem. But if they have made no attempt to pick out quotations for particular purposes, to illustrate particular points, then they will not 'know' the poem in a critical sense. Others may learn the whole poem in order to have a 'quotation bank' that they can use at will, and that could be useful if they have done the other work on it. But there are people who learn one poem and assume that the effort put into that is enough and they don't need to learn anything about any other poem. We have already seen how dangerous this can be if 'the' poem is not suitable for any of the questions.

Short stories come somewhere between novels and poems. The techniques of short story writing might have to be analysed closely, if the question asks for this, so you would need some detailed quotations to illustrate the techniques you might write about.

Key Points

Look back to Chapter 12 How Many Texts?

Multiply that number of texts by whatever you judge sufficient from Chapter 13 How Many Quotations?

That's your answer.

About 20–30 perhaps?

The bad news is that you now have to learn them.

The next bit of bad news is that you won't get to use them all.

Just as you have to **select** information and points to use for planning your essay, so you have to **select the appropriate quotations** for the line of thought suggested by the question you are answering. You won't necessarily use them all. Some of them may be irrelevant.

Just because you have learned a quotation, that doesn't mean that you have to use it.

Presenting Quotations

If the quotation you are using to illustrate a point is short, merely an expression like 'the cold stone parks', then you simply include the quotation in the sentence it belongs to. The same would normally be true of something less than a line of poetry. But if you have an extended quotation it is better to separate it out from the body of your answer by taking a new line and indenting the quotation:

Answer

Kath's letter to her mother created a storm of disapproval among her brothers and sisters. She wrote:

> 'I'll go with him and see what he's like as a man – and then marry him at leisure, if I feel in the mood. But he's hardly any money and we want to borrow some, so he and I are coming over on Sunday.'

This reveals important aspects of Kath's character by…

If your quotation is a complete line (or more) of poetry, you should quote it in its proper form, paying attention to the integrity of the lines. The poet wrote them that way so the least you can do is respect and follow the lineation.

Answer

The Duke makes his disapproval of his wife known to the visiting ambassador.

> 'She had
> A heart – how shall I say? – too soon made glad,
> Too easily impressed.'

This very chilling line reveals…

Common Mistakes

There is one more important point to watch when writing longer quotations. In both the examples above the comment after the quotation is a new sentence beginning with 'This'. Too often pupils go sailing on after a quotation to say 'this shows something important…' without noticing that they should have started a new sentence. This does their reputation for technical accuracy no good at all.

TIMING (CRITICAL ESSAY)

Using Your Time Well in the Exam

You have 1 hour 30 minutes for this paper.

There are 50 marks available.

You must answer *two* Critical Essay questions and 'each question is worth 25 marks'.

The number of marks is not really as important as it is in Paper 1 Close Reading where, as we have seen, you have to measure your time against the number of marks available for each question. However, it is important to notice two things:

1   Each question is worth the same, so each question should have equal time and attention.

2   Both questions together make up the same total as Paper 1, so this is equal in value, and needs just as much thinking and effort as Paper 1.

There is also the fact that we have to do some preparatory work on the Paper before we start answering questions.

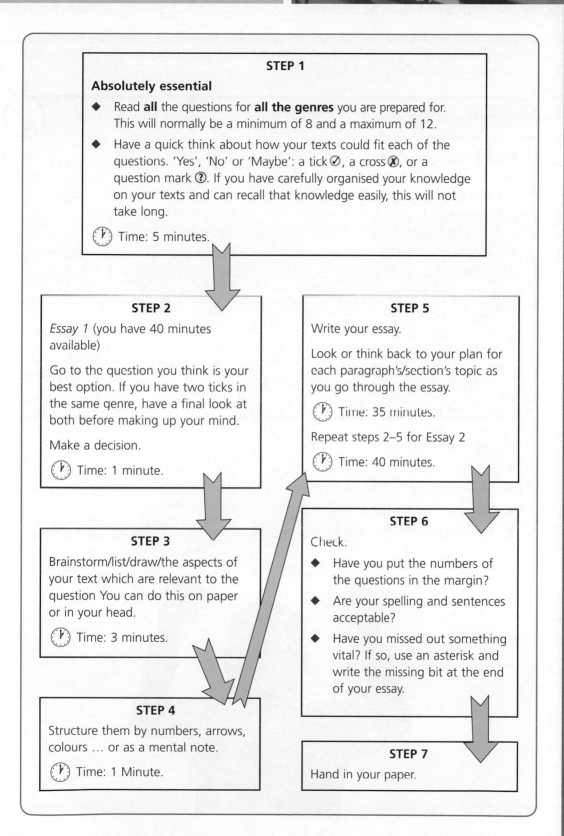

STEP 1

Absolutely essential

◆ Read **all** the questions for **all the genres** you are prepared for. This will normally be a minimum of 8 and a maximum of 12.

◆ Have a quick think about how your texts could fit each of the questions. 'Yes', 'No' or 'Maybe': a tick ⊘, a cross ⊗, or a question mark ⓘ. If you have carefully organised your knowledge on your texts and can recall that knowledge easily, this will not take long.

🕐 Time: 5 minutes.

STEP 2

Essay 1 (you have 40 minutes available)

Go to the question you think is your best option. If you have two ticks in the same genre, have a final look at both before making up your mind.

Make a decision.

🕐 Time: 1 minute.

STEP 3

Brainstorm/list/draw/the aspects of your text which are relevant to the question You can do this on paper or in your head.

🕐 Time: 3 minutes.

STEP 4

Structure them by numbers, arrows, colours … or as a mental note.

🕐 Time: 1 Minute.

STEP 5

Write your essay.

Look or think back to your plan for each paragraph's/section's topic as you go through the essay.

🕐 Time: 35 minutes.

Repeat steps 2–5 for Essay 2

🕐 Time: 40 minutes.

STEP 6

Check:

◆ Have you put the numbers of the questions in the margin?

◆ Are your spelling and sentences acceptable?

◆ Have you missed out something vital? If so, use an asterisk and write the missing bit at the end of your essay.

STEP 7

Hand in your paper.

But it might not happen like that. You will be rushing, the invigilator may have to prise your clenched hand off the paper, you have only done two thirds of your second essay and you still haven't checked your spelling!

Hints and Tips

Tips to Save Time

You can use your plan to help you to time your essay. How many numbers or headings do you have in your plan – 5? 7? You can check where you are after 20 minutes – have you reached point 3 or are you still at point 2? This will help you to see the need to push on – perhaps by missing something out – so that you can finish inside the time.

It is much better from the marks point of view to have two complete answers, rather than a long (possibly very good answer) and a half-finished one. If you take this to its logical conclusion and do one essay so well that you get the full 25 marks, but zero for the other, because you had barely started it, you could only get 25/50. With two less good but more complete answers you would get more marks.

This is a very panicky paper for a lot of people, because of the time restriction. But don't miss out on Steps 1 and 3. You should not start to write your first essay until at least 7 or 8 minutes have passed. Other people round about you may have written half a page by then. Don't panic, your approach is at least as good as, and probably better than, theirs.

You are now well-prepared:

◆ You know your texts.

◆ You know how to choose your questions.

◆ You can select the relevant material.

◆ Planning your structure and writing the essays should be a breeze.

PART 3

Writing

WRITING – THE FOLIO

Writing – The Task

You have to produce two pieces of writing for external assessment – that is, to be marked by SQA markers rather than by your own teacher. The writing process will be monitored by your teacher, and will have clearly defined stages, all of which have to be submitted:

◆ draft title and proposals

◆ outline plan

◆ first draft

◆ final version.

There are a number of other conditions to do with the production of your essays which your teacher or centre will tell you about. For example, you have to include the principal sources you have used to find material for your essay. This includes books, articles and websites. It is wise to remember that if you could find something on the internet, then so can the person who is marking your essay! This, along with other conditions, is to make sure that the writing is your own work. On top of that, you will be asked to sign a declaration stating that both pieces of writing are your own work before they are submitted to SQA.

One piece of writing must be what is broadly classed as 'Discursive':

◆ a persuasive essay

◆ an argumentative essay

◆ a report.

The other piece of writing must be what is broadly classed as 'Creative':

◆ a personal reflective essay

◆ a poem (or a set of linked poems)

◆ a piece of prose fiction

◆ a dramatic script.

In this section of the book we are going to concentrate on the most commonly produced types of essay: argumentative, persuasive, prose fiction, and personal reflective.

The Length

Each of the pieces submitted to SQA for external assessment must be at least 650 words long (except for poetry). On the other hand there is no point in writing at great length just for the sake of it – it often leads to rambling unfocused essays. The upper limit on each piece of work is 1300 words. Not sticking to these word limits will lead to your essays losing marks.

Writing – The Criteria

You will be familiar with the following already as they are the same criteria which you must meet in the piece of writing which is assessed internally in the course of your Language Unit.

What You Should Know

Content is relevant and appropriate for purpose and audience, reveals depth and complexity of thought and sustained development.

Structure is effective and appropriate for purpose, audience and genre; content is sequenced and organised in ways which assist impact.

Expression: capable use of techniques relevant to the genre and effective choice of words and sentence structure sustain a style and tone which clearly communicate a point of view/stance consistent with purpose and audience.

Technical Accuracy: spelling, grammar and punctuation are **consistently accurate**.

Although all the criteria above apply to all writing tasks, the importance of individual words and phrases vary according to the kind of writing you are attempting. We will look at these differences as we approach each particular type of writing.

The one which never varies and is always vitally important is the last one:

Technical Accuracy: spelling, grammar and punctuation are consistently accurate.

It is your responsibility to see that your essays meet this condition. If you can't write 'correct' English, then you will fail this part of the examination, and that will have an effect on your overall mark.

Discursive Writing

For discursive writing the most important words in the Performance Criteria are:

◆ depth and complexity of thought ◆ effective choice of words and sentence structure

◆ sustained development ◆ tone ◆ organised ◆ point of view/stance

An Argumentative Essay

This does not mean a quarrelsome essay! It means a piece which has an 'argument' in the same way that your Critical Essay has an 'argument' – a line of thought. There is a set of facts, views, evidence, judgments which you wish to communicate to someone else in order to inform them, enlighten them and make them think about the topic.

Of course, you have to find the content of your essay yourself: facts, evidence etc. In an argumentative essay you must consider at least two viewpoints, and treat each fairly. This does not mean your own personal preference has to be suppressed. You can be fair, but also very firm in your conclusion so long as it can be justified from the evidence you present.

A Persuasive Essay

If, on the other hand, there is a topic which simply makes your blood boil and you want to promote your viewpoint and convince your reader that you are 'right' then you are probably going to move into the sort of discursive writing described as 'persuasive'.

You may start with the same kind of content as for an argumentative essay, but you will use the material differently. You may suppress some evidence which does not suit your point of view, or, more skilfully, consider that evidence and then demolish it. Your conclusion will sound strong and irrefutable. The reader should be swept along by your argument and end up agreeing with you. Another approach is more subtle suggestion and quiet manipulation, where you use a rapier rather than a bludgeon. But the reader should still end up agreeing with you.

For Both Argumentative and Persuasive Essays

Check that your topic has the potential for stimulating deep and complex thought. Next, you can start assembling your material and working on a rough outline. You either already have, or will develop in the course of your research, a feeling for what you want to communicate to your reader. It is then time to produce your first draft. (Your centre will decide under what conditions you actually produce your first draft.)

This takes you through the first three steps of the procedure mentioned on page 172:

◆   draft title   ◆   outline plan   ◆   first draft.

After the first draft you then start on the real work, putting to use all that you have learned in other parts of your Higher English Course.

How Successful Is It as a Piece of Writing? How Can You Improve It?

The answers to these questions lie in your ability to analyse your own writing in the same way that you analyse writing in all the Close Reading practice you have been doing.

In all your discussions and practice dealing with Close Reading examples you have been looking at the techniques used by good discursive writers. Earlier in this book you have looked at extracts demonstrating the use of topic sentences (page 11); how points are made, (pages 18–22); how arguments are developed (pages 22–27) and in what ways links are effective (pages 32–35). There is also a section about the effectiveness of a conclusion on pages 91–93.

You should be able to apply the same close inspection to your own work. For each paragraph:

◆   What is the topic?

◆   What are the points being made?

◆   How does the paragraph help to develop the overall argument?

◆   How does each paragraph link with the next in a logical way?

And for the whole essay:

◆   How does the overall structure of the essay promote your conclusion?

You can get even closer than that. On page 44 you looked at the words 'reeked' and 'drippingly'. The writer's choice of words with resonant connotations helps to make the point. Look again at how images work – 'twisty ruler' and 'giant squid', for example (page 48). Sentence structure is also something which you have looked at closely. Look back to page 60 – you will see how an effective and clear sentence structure helps to carry and clarify the writer's meaning. All that you have learned about word choice, imagery and sentence structure can help you to analyse your own writing to make it more effective.

Hints and Tips

All this work should be carefully completed before you submit your final draft. There is no point in producing draft after draft, each marginally different from the one before, and indeed your centre will not allow you to do this. There will be a limit to the number of times you can submit your essay, and you don't want to squander any of them.

Check: Spelling, grammar and punctuation are consistently accurate.

Practice in Writing Discursive Essays

A source for practice material can be found almost anywhere where two writers deal with the same subject but from different viewpoints. In the Opinion section of the *Sunday Herald*, for example, almost every week there is a feature which gives two views to a topical question such as 'Are our pets destroying the planet?' or 'Are computer games destroying family life?' In the *Observer* (New Review section) there are sometimes similar Yes and No articles, for example, 'Would France be right to restrict wearing the burka in public?'

These articles can give you practice in three ways:

1 Try organising the material into a well-balanced argument with a logical conclusion.

2 Use the material to write a persuasive essay coming down totally on one side or the other, selecting and slanting some of the points from both articles.

3 Use the material to practise for the **Question on both passages** section of the Close Reading Paper. You can use an all-purpose question such as 'Which is the more convincing/effective in ideas or style, or both?'

Creative Writing

Remember to consider the important words for this genre: relevance, depth and complexity of thought, and sustained development. But add to that: effective structure, use of techniques relevant to the genre, effective choice of words…

Prose Fiction

Over your school career you have probably read at least 50 short stories. It is likely that you have carefully analysed a number of these in the last two or three years. The discussions and essays based on fiction which you have experienced in the run up to your Higher Course will have homed in on a number of common features: plot, structure, setting, characterisation…

You will find a full selection of these features on page 114. Ideally, you should be able to look at your own work in the light of the same analytical techniques which you have applied to the work of professional writers.

But all this depends on your having written a short story in the first place! It is not easy. The weakest aspect of most short stories presented at Higher level is plotting. There are many promising openings, lots of subtle characterisation, atmospheric settings, tension or suspense, but quite often this leads to a predictable, banal or an impossible ending – even the old cop-out (the equivalent of the primary school ending) – 'I woke up and it was all a dream!'

Plots have to do more than carry the story, they should also allow the theme(s) to emerge. How will the reader's understanding of the human condition be enlarged by your story?

We will suppose that you have a plot outline, a draft title (you may change this for something more dramatic once you have finished the story) and that you have written the first draft of your story. (Your centre will decide under what conditions you produce your first draft.)

Again, you will have fulfilled the requirements:

◆ draft title   ◆ outline plan   ◆ first draft.

This is only the very first stage. Editing comes next. This can involve taking out unnecessary detail, substituting more effective words, clarifying your sentence structure, seeding hints, changing the order of words, sentences or paragraphs to achieve, for example, maximum tension, humour, emotional charge…

The following example comes from the beginning of a short story 'The Actor' by Stan Barstow. Just after these events, Albert is persuaded to take the small part of a policeman in the local dramatic society's production of a domestic drama 'The Son of the House'.

Example 1

He was a big man, without surplus flesh, and with an impassivity of face that hid extreme shyness, and which, allied with his striking build, made him look more than anything else, as he walked homewards in the early evening in fawn mackintosh and trilby hat, like a plain-clothes policeman going quietly and efficiently about his business, with trouble for someone at the end of it.

All his adult life people had been saying to him, 'You should have been a policeman, Mr Royston,' or, more familiarly, 'You've missed your way Albert. You're cut out for a copper, lad.' But he would smile in his quiet patient way, as though no one had ever said it before, and almost always gave exactly the same reply: 'Nay, I'm all right. I like my bed at nights.'

In reality he was a shop assistant and could be found, in a white smock, on five and a half days of the week behind the counter of the Moorend branch grocery store of Cressley Industrial Cooperative Society, where he was assistant manager. He had been assistant manager for five years and seemed fated to occupy that position for many more years to come before the promotion earmarked for him would become a fact, for the manager was a man of settled disposition also, and comparatively young and fit.

But Albert did not apparently worry. He did not apparently worry about anything; but this again was the deception of his appearance. Quiet he might be, and stolid and settled in his ways; but no one but he had known the agony of shyness that was his wedding day; and no one but he had known the pure terror of the premature birth of his only child, when the dead baby he longed for with so much secret yearning had almost cost him the life of the one person without whom his life would hardly have been possible – Alice, his wife.

So it was the measure of his misleading appearance and his ability to hide his feelings that no one ever guessed the truth, that no one was ever led from the belief that he was a taciturn man of unshakeable placidity. 'You want to take a leaf out of Albert's book,' they would say. 'Take a lesson from him. Never worries, Albert doesn't.'

Thus Albert, at the age of thirty-seven, on the eve of his small adventure.

This beginning, along with the **title** 'The Actor', points towards something happening, possibly during a performance of the play, which will reinforce our impression of Albert's character as we have it here, or which will possibly transform his character completely.

Characterisation gives us an impression of him right from the beginning. What stands out is the discrepancy between the personality suggested by his outward appearance, and the sensitiveness of his inner self. The physical description is given in detail – his face, clothes, build and manner. Normally one of the faults of weaker stories is too much unnecessary description – it usually doesn't matter whether the heroine is blond or brunette, tall or short, but the irrelevant details are often recorded nonetheless. In *this* story, however, the description of Albert's exterior is essential because it contrasts with the inner man.

The **setting** – Cressley, Moorend, the Industrial Cooperative Society – is sketched in lightly, just enough to suggest a sort of monotonous, rather mundane kind of existence.

The **structure** is carefully crafted to give us a defined and intriguing beginning to the story. The last three paragraphs of the opening begin with the words, 'But', 'So', 'Thus' leading to the real heart of the adventure which will be central to the story as a whole: 'Thus Albert…'

Details of **effective word choice** are everywhere. Look especially at 'apparently' and its repetition. Look at 'agony', 'pure terror', 'secret yearning'.

The **odd word order of the sentence** 'Quiet he might be…' puts the important thing first; the repeated 'and' adds to this outward picture which is so at odds with the inner insecurities.

Hints and Tips

You should apply all these tests to your own writing in order to improve it. There is no point in handing in another draft until you have worked on it extensively and you are satisfied with it. And there is no point in refining it endlessly if your initial plot is weak – start again.

Check: Spelling, grammar and punctuation are consistently accurate.

The form of short story discussed above is that most commonly studied, but there are many others (e.g. post-modernist, stream of consciousness…) which you can attempt – especially if you have discussed and practised them. You can also try other forms of prose fiction – a chapter from a novel, for instance, but the same analytical procedure as above applies.

Personal Reflective

What You Should Know

These are the two most important statements about personal reflective writing:

1. 'This writing will aim to interest or give pleasure, rather than simply to convey information; it will concern itself usually with a single **idea**, **insight** or **experience** and will include reflection on **knowledge**, **thoughts** or **feelings** engendered by it.'

2. 'The reflective essay at Higher is not simply an account of an experience.'

Most commonly the words from the statements above which are paired together are:

◆ '…single **experience** and will include reflection on **feelings** engendered' and the tone adopted is often sad or anguished.

But there are lots of other approaches possible:

◆ '…a single **idea** and will include reflection on **thoughts** engendered…' dealt with in a whimsical or humorous tone e.g., an essay on handbags and their centrality to self-image; or the trauma caused by separation from your life support system – your iPhone.

◆ '…single **insight** and will include reflection on **knowledge** engendered…' dealt with in concerned or contemplative tone e.g., an insight into the nature of an aspect of society and the enlarging sense of understanding stemming from the knowledge gained.

The weakest essays simply describe a sad event in great detail, with an added-on reflective paragraph about the lessons learned from the experience. This kind of essay will struggle to pass.

Remember to consider the important words for this genre:

◆ **relevance, depth and complexity of thought**

◆ **clearly communicate a point of view/sense of the writer's personality**

◆ **appropriate tone, effective structure, effective choice of words…**

Ask yourself the following questions before you start:

◆ Can I isolate an idea or insight or experience I feel is important enough to write about?

◆ How has reflection on this idea or insight or experience added to my understanding (of myself, or of others, or of life, the universe and everything…)?

Now all you have to do is find a provisional title; write an outline; and then your first draft. (Your centre will decide under what conditions you actually produce your first draft.)

The advice on editing your first draft is almost exactly the same as that given for the short story (above pages 176-177). This can involve taking out unnecessary detail, substituting more effective words, clarifying your sentence structure, changing the order of words, sentences or paragraphs to achieve, for example, maximum tension, humour, emotional charge…

Apply the same tests as you would to a piece of fiction you have studied for Critical Essay, or approach your own writing as if it were a piece of Textual Analysis. In either case the important question is – is it effective? And when you are satisfied with your final draft…

Check: Spelling, grammar and punctuation are consistently accurate.

Finally, a Word about Poetry and Dramatic Scripts

Poetry

This specialist writing form should be practised a great deal before presenting anything for assessment. Some splendid examples are seen, but there is also some very weak work. Probably the most common weakness is in form. Quite often the ideas, imagery and word choice are effective and striking, but there is a weak structure. Lines seem to occur randomly, without reason. What may be presented as 'free verse' is often simply poetic prose set out in lines.

Dramatic Scripts

This specialist form has its own conventions and rules. There is the problem of plotting (see comments on the short story, page 175) and of carrying that plot, and the characterisation necessary to support it, in dialogue/monologue. The most common fault is to produce lines which don't sound convincing for the character and to overburden the piece with stage directions as a substitute for character interaction. But, in the right hands, good pieces are possible.